Copyright © 2025 Jyllip Corp.

All rights reserved. No part of this book may be reproduced or used in any manner without the prior written permission of the copyright owner, except for the use of brief quotations in a book review.

Paperback ISBN: 978-1-0690430-3-0
eBook ISBN: 978-1-0690430-1-6

Design by Jason Arias

Printed in the United States of America

Inside Google Ads

FIRST EDITION

Everything You
Need to Know About
Audience Targeting

JYLL SASKIN GALES

For Nora Mercer,
my favourite girl in the whole wide world
I love you forever

Contents

Foreword XIII

What is audience targeting? 1
  Audience vs. content targeting 1
    ☑ Remember this! Audience vs. Content targeting 3

What are your Audience Targeting options in Google Ads? 5
  Your data aka Remarketing 6
    Your website data 8
      Dynamic remarketing 9
    Your app data 10
    Your Google content 12
      YouTube remarketing 12
      Engaged audiences 15
    Your customer data 17

What you need to know about Customer Match	18
Features enabled by Customer Match	20
Account eligibility	21
List formatting	22
List size	22
Customer Match policies	24
Remember this! Four types of Your data segments in Google Ads	24
Limitations on Remarketing	25
List size	25
Personalized advertising policies	25
Cheat Sheet: Your data segments	27
Google's data	28
Detailed demographics	29
Affinity segments	33
In-Market segments	34

Life events	36
☑ Remember this! Four types of audience segments based on Google's data	37
Cheat Sheet: Google's Data	38
A combination of your data and Google's data	39
Custom segments	40
How to use Custom segments	42
Custom interests, Custom search terms and Search themes	46
Musings & Predictions for Custom segments	50
Tips for success with Custom segments	51
☑ Remember this! Four ways to build a Custom segment	56
Combined segments	57
How to use Combined segments	60
Combined segments vs. Custom combination segments	62
Audience Builder	65
Musings & Predictions for Combined segments	69
Tips for success with Combined segments: Audience layering	70
☑ Remember this! Custom vs. Combined segments	77
Cheat Sheet: Combining your data and Google's data	78
Automated targeting	80
Optimized targeting	81
Audience expansion	84
Audience signal	86
Search themes	90
Keyword prioritization and Search themes	94
Lookalike segments	97
What happened to Similar segments?	103
App campaigns (Exclusion only)	104

☐ Remember this! Types of automated targeting in Google Ads 105
Cheat Sheet: Automated targeting 106

How to use audiences in your Google Ads campaigns 109
  Display, Video and Demand Gen campaigns 109
    Display and Video campaigns 110
    Demand Gen campaigns 111
      Google-owned properties 112
      Demand Gen vs. Display campaigns 113
    Audience compatibility with Display, Video and Demand Gen campaigns 115
    Audience attribution hierarchy 116
  Search & Shopping campaigns 117
    Audience compatibility with Search and Shopping campaigns 118
    Targeting vs. Observation 118
      ☐ Remember this! Targeting mode vs. Observation mode 120
    Remarketing Lists for Search Ads (RLSA) 120
  Performance Max campaigns 122
    ☐ Remember this! Audience targeting vs. Audience signal 123
    ☐ Remember this! Search keywords vs. Search themes 123
  App campaigns 124
    ☐ Remember this! Google Ads campaign types 126
  Audience insights 126

How audiences work with... 133
  How audiences work with bidding 134
    ☐ Remember this! Smart Bidding strategies 135
  How audiences work with creative 135

How audiences work with conversion tracking	137
Conversion-based customer lists	138
How to build an effective audience strategy	143
Audience exclusion as a strategy	147
Non-Linear Targeting	147
B2B Targeting	150
Your targeting strategy template	154
Privacy, cookies & industry changes	157
Cookies & Pixels 101	159
☑ Remember this: Cookie vs. Pixel	160
The problem with cookies	160
How to win with Google Ads today	161
☑ Remember this! 3 durable ways to outsmart your competitors in Google Ads	162
Inside Google Ads AI policy	164
Acknowledgements	166

Foreword

IT'S 8:30ᴾᴹ **ON** June 20, 2022.

Today is my parents' 46th wedding anniversary, and I'm sitting on the couch in their living room. The lights are out, and the summer sun is setting.

It's quiet. My parents are sleeping, and my daughter is sleeping in the next room, too.

A few days ago, my husband got back from a trip and tested positive for COVID, so my daughter and I immediately moved in with my parents for 10 days. A great anniversary present, right? None of us had gotten the virus yet, and we wanted to keep that winning streak.

If I were sitting on the couch in my house at 8:30pm, I would pour a glass of wine, open up some chips or chocolate (or both), scroll mindlessly through TikTok for a few hours, and stagger to bed once I couldn't keep my eyes open anymore. Standard pandemic-era evening routine.

But at my parents' place, I didn't have my usual snacks in the cupboard. I couldn't be too loud, or I'd wake someone up. I was secretly jabbing myself with needles morning and night, preparing for a scheduled embryo transfer in 10 days, so I was feeling like crap and trying desperately to hide it. Oh, and I wasn't drinking. What the heck was I supposed to do?

For some mysterious reason, I got the urge to write a book.

It had been just 4 months since I launched my membership course, Inside Google Ads. The most recent lesson I'd filmed was called "All about audiences," so audience targeting was fresh on my mind, and I felt like I had a lot more to say.

Over the next 10 days, I wrote 33 pages.

Then, my husband was COVID-free, we moved back into our home, and my book writing urge left as fast as it came.

I'm happy to say that the embryo transfer was successful, and I found out I was pregnant. Months flew by and time ceased to have much meaning. My daughter started kindergarten, I gave birth to my son, I went on maternity leave, we moved houses, I launched 2 more courses, then started a podcast… life happened and business kept moving. The unfinished audience targeting manuscript sat untouched for 2 years, collecting dust on the proverbial Google Docs shelf.

But I kept thinking about this book. I *needed* to share this with you, in a format where we could dive deep and explore and analyze and hypothesize. A respite from the "hot takes" and "unpopular opinions" we constantly craft to appease the social media algorithms. No hooks or engagement bait, no dealing with trolls in the comments, just some wholesome nerding out over Google Ads minutiae. Practical, useful information.

FOREWORD

Well, the fact that you're reading this right now means I did it. I wrote the damn thing. And you bought the damn thing. And here we are!

This book is for the Google Ads practitioner who wants to understand *how* and *why* things work the way they do. Whether you're a business owner, a freelancer, an in-house marketer, an agency employee, a student, a Googler or simply a PPC enthusiast, my goal is to deepen your *appreciation* of audience targeting. To get you better results from your Google Ads, of course, but also to understand the nuances, the intricacies and even the contradictions inherent in Google Ads audience targeting.

There are a few expectations I'd like to set about what you will and will not find in this book, and then we'll dive into the main event.

Within *Inside Google Ads*, you will not find tactical information about App campaigns nor specialized campaign types like Hotel ads, Things to do ads, Vehicle ads, etc. I know a lot about a lot of things, but I know very little about App campaigns, and virtually nothing about industry-specific campaign types. For your benefit, and mine, I'll stick to writing about what I know. We'll touch on App campaigns a few times as they fit into the overall audience targeting picture, but that's it.

Next, I take my role as a trusted Google Ads coach, teacher and content creator very seriously. *Inside Google Ads* is a thoroughly fact-checked resource on how things work in Google Ads right now. That being said, Google is constantly changing, which is why you'll see that the cover of this book says "First Edition." By the time you're reading this, it's inevitable that something will have been deprecated, or changed names, or altered in some way. As I'm writing, I am verifying all of my factual statements about how things work with:

- multiple Google Ads accounts, across industries, countries and sizes

- the Google Ads Help Center
- and where the first two conflict, Ginny Marvin, Ads Product Liaison at Google, has graciously clarified and verified my questions

I will be clear with you when we are departing from facts and "how things work" into my own predictions and musings. I will also be very clear when something is an "official Google explanation," and when something is "Jyll language" or "the way I prefer to explain."

Next, because of how quickly things change in Google Ads, I decided not to include screenshots in this book. Instead, as a book reader, **you can use the code BOOKONE to get 50% off your first month of access to my *Inside Google Ads* course** at learn.jyll.ca. Yup, really! I've set up a section in my course especially for book readers, with video tutorials and cheat sheets and all the resources you need to complement what you're about to read here. You can cancel your *Inside Google Ads* subscription at any time. If you don't cancel, you'll be charged the regular monthly price from your second month onwards.

Additionally, you won't find anything AI-generated in this book. I wrote this book 100% with my brain, it was edited 100% with my brain and the kind brains of fellow humans, and it was designed 100% by a human. No AI tools were used in any part of the book creation process. I care about this deeply, and I've included the "Inside Google Ads AI Policy" at the end of this book if you'd like to learn more.

Finally, you won't find any complaining about Google in *Inside Google Ads*. Am I going to constantly fawn over my former employer and wax rhapsodic about the innovation and power of the big G? No. But am I going to moan about how we're losing control and transparency

FOREWORD

and Google only cares about making money and nothing else? Also no.

In this book, you'll find fair criticism, measured optimism, and some gentle poking fun at Google Ads product decisions that I find questionable. My mantra is to work with the system, not against the system, to drive the best results for your business. I've written this book for you so that you can get the might of Google working for your business, too.

And now, dear reader, let us step out into the night and pursue that flighty temptress, adventure.

What is audience targeting?

AUDIENCE TARGETING IS showing ads to people based on *who they are*.

That probably sounds very basic. Why *wouldn't* you show ads to people based on who they are?

Why did you buy a whole book about such a simple concept?

But if you think back 20 years or so, it was not normal at all. Offline media, like print, broadcast and out-of-home - none of them used audience targeting, because they couldn't.

In fact, throughout 99% of the history of advertising, we've relied on content targeting: showing ads based on *what people are engaging with*.

Audience vs. content targeting

Let's say you decide to advertise your business in the infamous September issue of Vogue magazine. You have some idea about the kinds of people who might be reading Vogue, and you think those people overlap with your target audience. Perhaps the print readership of Vogue is predominantly female, 50+, high net worth and interested in fashion.

Once you place that ad and it runs in the magazine, *every single person* who reads the September issue of Vogue will have the opportunity to see your ad. That's what makes this content targeting, you are showing your ad to *people who are reading the September issue of Vogue magazine.*

Content targeting doesn't mean you're not taking the intended audience into account. It means that you're picking that specific content, that physical real estate in that magazine, because you have data about the types of people who are likely to engage with it. However, anyone who picks up that magazine can see that ad, regardless of who they are.

Now, many of those people will be in your ideal audience. That's why the advertising industry has always worked this way. But your ad won't *only* show to your ideal audience. Other people who will see your ad might include a kid picking up that Vogue a few months later while waiting for a doctor's appointment. A teenage girl who dreams of moving to New York City and devours every issue. A spouse who's bored while sitting on the toilet and picks up that Vogue sitting on the counter. They are all consuming the same content, so they all get the same ads.

Content targeting isn't some archaic, offline media relic, though. Content targeting exists and thrives in digital channels, too. In fact, the bread and butter of Google Ads - Search campaigns - are based on a type of content targeting: keywords. You pick specific keywords, which you believe will match to what your ideal audience is searching for. You launch your campaign. Assuming you have sufficient budget, bids and quality to do so, you can show an ad to every single person whose searches match your keywords, regardless of who they are. They're searching for your keywords, they can see your ads. Content targeting.

You can also run your Display campaigns or Video campaigns with content targeting, by picking specific Topics, Placements or Keywords for your ads. For example, you may want to show ads to people when they are watching YouTube videos about exercise, or when they are reading articles that mention money-saving grocery shopping tips, or when they're playing Candy Crush.

We'll explore content targeting again throughout this book, since it often complements audience targeting strategies. But for now, we're going to dive down deep into audience targeting, how it works, and what your options are in Google Ads.

☐ Remember this! Audience vs. Content targeting

Audience targeting means showing ads *to* certain types of *PEOPLE*

Content targeting means showing ads *in* certain types of *PLACES*

What are your Audience Targeting options in Google Ads?

THERE ARE INFINITE ways to reach your ideal customers using Google's convoluted web of audience targeting capabilities. They fall into four categories.

The four types of audience targeting you can use, in Google Ads or any ad platform:
1. Your data
2. Google's data (or the platform's data)
3. A combination of your data and Google's data
4. Automated targeting

When we talk about audience targeting, we are usually talking about inclusion. By adding audience segments to your campaigns or ad groups, you are telling Google who you'd like It to *include* in your ad targeting.

Many audiences can also be used for exclusion, to tell Google who you *don't want to show ads to*. As we explore each type, I'll clarify when and how you can use each audience type for inclusion or exclusion.

Your data aka Remarketing

The first audience targeting category is what you would typically call remarketing or retargeting. In Google Ads, it's called Your data segments. This is when you show ads to *people who've interacted with your business before*. It's one of the most common and generally most profitable paid ads tactics.

I like the name "remarketing" because it perfectly describes what you're doing here; you are re + marketing, you are marketing again, you are showing ads to someone that your business already knows. For the rest of this book, I'll use the term "remarketing" to refer to this audience targeting tactic, and the term "Your data segments" when I'm specifically referring to implementing your remarketing strategies within Google Ads.

If you're a Meta Ads practitioner, you can think of Your data segments as equivalent to Custom audiences. However, be forewarned: Custom segments, which used to be called Custom audiences, refer to something completely different in Google Ads, and we'll get to that when we explore the third type of audience targeting: a combination of your data and Google's data.

Within Your data segments, there are four different kinds of remarketing you can do. While these are the categories you'll find in Google Ads, the capabilities are very similar regardless of which ad platform you're using.

The four types of remarketing you can use in Google Ads are based on people who:

1. Visited your **website**
2. Used your **app**
3. Interacted with your **Google** content
4. Gave you their contact information, like an **email address**

These remarketing segments are all managed in the Google Ads interface by navigating to Tools > Shared Library > Audience Manager.

In Audience Manager, you'll find all the remarketing segments in your account under Your data segments (it's the first tab). These segments will be categorized by whether they are currently being used by your campaigns, or not being used by your campaigns. You can also see the approximate size of each segment, whether they're eligible to serve, and where they're eligible to serve (Search, Display, YouTube, etc.)

Depending on your strategy, you may want to exclude remarketing segments rather than targeting them. For example, some businesses don't want to show ads to people who've recently purchased, so you could add Your data segments as exclusions to a Search, Display, Demand Gen or Video campaign. You can do this by navigating on the left-hand sidebar to Audiences, keywords, and content > Audiences and scrolling down. Underneath the section where you *add* your audience segments, you'll find the area where you can *exclude* audience segments.

Note that you cannot exclude audience segments from Shopping campaigns.

Remarketing is still one of those things that makes me think, "I can't believe we can do this." How lucky as we, as marketers, that we can not only use infinite ad targeting methods to reach our ideal customers, but we can also craft messages explicitly for those who have interacted with our business before? And if they leave our "digital storefront" (aka our website) without making a purchase, we can find them and show ads to them again and again and again? We take this for granted now, especially as consumers. *Why are those dang shoes following me across the internet?!* And with the degradation of third-party cookie data (yup, we'll get there before this book is finished), it's true that website-based remarketing is no longer as accurate as it used to be. There are also policy restrictions in place that limit when and where remarketing can be used. I'm not trying to tamp down on your excitement for remarketing, just set realistic expectations. Remarketing is fabulous - with caveats.

Let's explore those four types of remarketing in greater detail, and then we'll discuss those limitations, some caveats, and my tips for success with Your data segments.

Your website data

The most common type of remarketing is to show ads to *people who have visited your website*. After all, if someone has already been to your website, that means they've not only heard of you before, but they're also interested in what you offer and have taken the time to "check you out."

You can set up website remarketing using Google Analytics or the Google tag. Setting up remarketing using Google Analytics is easier, since most businesses using Google Ads already have Google Analytics set up on their website. First, you'll need to link Google Analytics to your Google Ads account. Then, it just takes a few clicks to create Audiences in Google Analytics, and a few more clicks to import them into Google Ads from Audience Manager.

However, remarketing using the Google tag is better because it's more accurate, more flexible, more timely, more comprehensive... all that good stuff. The biggest drawback, of course, is that Google Tag Manager can be confusing, finicky, and complicated, especially if you've never used it before.

Google Analytics remarketing is perfectly sufficient for most small businesses; it is far better to have remarketing set up via Google Analytics than no remarketing at all. If you have the capability to set up the Google tag on your website, or the budget to hire a consultant to do so, that's a good idea - especially for conversion tracking purposes.

When you're setting up a remarketing list to use for ad targeting, you'll want to consider two key things, and name your segments accordingly:

1. What kind of users do I want on my list?
2. For how long should they stay on my list?

The most common starting point is an All Users (30 days) segment. As you might have guessed, that's a remarketing segment that contains everyone who has visited your website within the last 30 days. From there, you might add an All Users (90 days) segment, to keep track of people who have visited your website within a longer timeframe. Perhaps you'll also add something like Product Viewers (7 days), for everyone who has viewed one of your products over the last week, or Pricing Page Viewers (28 days), for everyone who has made it to your pricing selection page over the last 4 weeks. The opportunities are endless; you can create as many remarketing segments as you'd like.

Dynamic remarketing

Dynamic remarketing is a special kind of website remarketing that tailors ads to users who've visited your website *based on which products or services they've viewed.*

You know those shoes you viewed last week that seem to be following you across the internet? That's dynamic remarketing. Rather than showing you a generic ad with top selling products, for example, the ad is tailored to show you the products you viewed, like a specific pair of shoes.

To set up dynamic remarketing, you'll need to create a feed. A feed is a collection of data, formatted in a way that Google Ads can understand. It can simply be a basic spreadsheet with a few columns. The most common type of feed you'll encounter is a shopping feed created in Google Merchant Center, the part of Google that stores product information from your store. A shopping feed is necessary to run a Shopping campaign in Google Ads, too.

Fun fact: You don't need to sell products through an online store in order to use dynamic remarketing. For example, if you sell travel products like flights, hotels or packages, you would definitely want to remarket to people who were interested in a certain destination on certain dates, but didn't book yet. If you work in the real estate industry, you can remarket to people who've shown interest in certain houses or apartments. You can create a custom feed for any type of business!

Once you have a feed in place, you may also need to set up other parameters and settings for dynamic remarketing to work. Google has a ton of resources on this in the Google Ads Help Center, and there are plenty of free tutorials available online as well. Even if you use a store platform like Shopify, for example, which connects your store quite seamlessly to Google Merchant Center and Google Ads for you, you still may need to tweak a few things to get dynamic remarketing working properly.

Your app data

Remarketing to *people who've used your app* works very similarly to remarketing to people who've visited your website.

First, you'll need to link your Firebase account or your approved third-party app analytics platform to Google Ads as a data source. Then, you can choose which in-app actions will cause users to be added to your audience segment. For example, users who visit a certain screen, click a certain button, make an in-app purchase - whatever you'd like to track.

When creating a new app-based segment, you can either start with an empty segment, or you can pre-fill the segment with users who've matched the audience requirements within the last 30 days.

- *Starting with an empty segment* means your segment will only start collecting users once it's created. You'll start with 0 users on your list, and you'll need to wait until you have sufficient users before you can use this segment in your campaign targeting.
- *Pre-filling your segment* means that instead of starting with 0 users, Google will look at the list criteria and automatically add all users who *would have met the criteria* over the last 30 days. This means you can add the audience segment to your campaign and start showing ads to relevant users right away, assuming that enough people have met the list requirements over the last 30 days.

Neither choice is right nor wrong, it simply depends on what you're trying to achieve. For example, if you want to show ads to users who interacted with your app after a certain update, starting with an empty segment will likely be the right choice. However, if you want to show ads to users who added something to their cart in-app but didn't complete the purchase, pre-filling the segment will likely be the better option for you, so you can ramp up your campaign quickly.

Your Google content

Website remarketing lets you show ads to people who've interacted with your website. App remarketing lets you show ads to people who've interacted with your app. Accordingly, Google remarketing lets you show ads to *people who've interacted with your content on Google* - both your organic content and your ads.

It's worth noting that every online advertising platform lets you do something similar to this: remarketing to people who've interacted with *your* content on *their* platform. In Meta Ads, you can remarket to people who've interacted with your Facebook or Instagram content. In LinkedIn Ads, you can remarket to people who've interacted with your LinkedIn content. In TikTok Ads, you can remarket to people who've interacted with your TikTok content. And on and on. Most platforms call this a Custom segment or Custom audience, but the term "Custom segment" actually means something completely different in Google Ads. (We'll get to that later.)

There are two types of Your data segments you can use based on user engagement with your Google content: YouTube remarketing and Google Engaged audiences.

YouTube remarketing
Some people consider YouTube to be a social media platform. Others think of it more like a search engine; the second largest search engine

in the world, in fact, after Google Search itself. Whatever you call it, YouTube remarketing is an effective and often-overlooked audience strategy.

Because YouTube is owned by Google, YouTube is tightly integrated with Google Ads, which makes YouTube remarketing one of the *easiest* types of Your data segments to set up. You don't need to connect your website to Google Analytics or add the Google tag, you don't need to connect your app to Firebase or some third-party platform. YouTube and Google are family, they already speak the same language.

This makes YouTube remarketing not only one of the easiest to activate, but also the most *accurate* type of remarketing. Since it's not reliant on third-party cookies or complicated integrations to work, you can "capture" virtually everyone who's engaged with your YouTube content on your YouTube remarketing segments. (You'll see shortly that Engaged audiences share this benefit, too.)

In order to show ads to people who've interacted with your YouTube content, you'll need to link your YouTube channel to Google Ads. This is usually a straightforward process. The part that trips some people up is you need to be an Owner of your YouTube channel in order to link it to Google Ads. If you're not connecting your own channel, you may need to get your client on the phone to help you complete this process for the accounts they own.

Once the YouTube channel and Google Ads account are linked, you can build a Your data segment in Audience Manager based on people who:
- Viewed any video
- Viewed certain videos
- Viewed any video (as an ad)
- Viewed certain videos as ads
- Subscribed

- Visited the channel page
- Liked any video
- Added any video to a playlist
- Shared any video

Recently, Google added a new capability to YouTube remarketing segments, which you'll definitely want to try if creators often make videos about your business. You can now build an audience segment based off of people who've interacted with videos *from another YouTube channel*, as long as you establish a link between that channel and your Google Ads account (which requires authorization from that channel owner). This is great for UGC, product reviews, sponsorship deals, etc.

Even if you're not sure whether or not you'll want to use the audience of other channels' videos for ad targeting purposes, it's a good idea to start this conversation with creators, see if they're open to the possibility, and establish expectations around potential compensation for them.

As with any remarketing list, when you create a data segment based off of YouTube users, you'll need to choose the Membership Duration: how long someone stays on the list. The default is 30 days, and the maximum is 540 days. Depending on the list type and planned campaign objective, I usually choose a duration between 30-90 days. For most businesses, anything shorter than 30 days will likely have too few users on it, and anything longer than 90 days... well, can you remember anything about the YouTube videos you watched 3 months ago?

As with app-based segments, YouTube-based segments allow you to pre-fill your segment from the last 30 days. When you set up most types of remarketing lists, in Google or other ad platforms, the list only starts collecting data once it's created. That means the list starts out empty, so it can take some time before you can use it in your campaigns. That's why it's handy that Google Ads lets you pre-fill your YouTube segments, because it means you can start using the list right away in a campaign rather than waiting for it to populate. If you don't want to pre-fill your YouTube user list, simply choose "Start with an empty segment."

Engaged audiences
The newest type of Your data segment in Google Ads is called Engaged audiences. This segment type is such an elegant solution to a complicated problem, it brought a genuine smile to my face when I first started seeing Engaged audiences pop up in my clients' accounts.

Engaged audiences let you reach users who have previously interacted with your website on Google Search, YouTube, Maps, and other Google properties. Every Google Ads account automatically gets one Engaged audience segment, and this segment will automatically populate with users who have visited your site from Google properties, through either ads or organic search result clicks. No account linking or audience setup necessary!

What makes Engaged audiences special?
- *Ease of use*. Unlike every other type of remarketing, you don't need to do anything. No Google tag. No account linking. No data uploads. An Engaged audience segment will magically appear in your Google Ads account, and you can use it with just a few clicks.
- *Simplicity*. Every Google Ads account gets one Engaged audience, and this segment will include everyone who

visited your website from your Google Ads on Google-owned properties, and from organic search results on Google. While I'm sure people are already complaining about this "limitation," wishing for landing page segmentation and property segmentation, I view this as a "feature" - Engaged audiences exist to help small business owners, and small business owners don't need more bells and whistles.
- *First-party data.* Since Engaged audiences populate with users who are on a Google-owned property, and then click to your website, Google knows exactly who those users are. As with YouTube-based remarketing segments, these are mostly signed-in users, so audience quality is high and there's no need to pass data back and forth.

This is what makes Engaged audiences such an elegant solution. Google is already tracking when people click from an ad to your website. Rather than waiting until they land on your website, and then tracking them through cookies or some other technology you need to implement and maintain, Google is now capturing their information *before* they leave Google Search, YouTube, etc. - and since these sites are all part of Google's ecosystem, Google takes care of user consent and tracking, and you now have an easy-to-use remarketing solution.

The challenge with Engaged audiences is that it's *only* tracking people who clicked on your ads or search results. Depending on your budget and overall marketing strategy, this may be a small portion of your total website visitors. If you're also running Meta Ads, for example, people who visit your website from Meta Ads would not be tracked by your Google Engaged audience. If you have a lot of direct traffic, or organic social media traffic, or referral traffic, those website visitors would not be included on your Engaged audience segment either.

Google recommends implementing Engaged audiences alongside your existing remarketing solutions, and I support that recommendation. But if you're reading this as someone who has *no* remarketing implemented, Engaged audiences are your game-changer.

Your customer data

Bringing your own customer data into Google Ads enables the most powerful type of remarketing. In the marketing industry, we refer to your customer list as first-party data because it has data that you directly collected from your customers: their names, email addresses, phone numbers and/or mailing addresses.

This is why seemingly every website prompts you to sign up for their email list in exchange for 10% off your purchase; they know how powerful it is to be able to collect your data and start building a direct relationship with you.

While all four types of remarketing in Google Ads involve using your data, the other types rely on your data that lives within the Google ecosystem. For example, if you create a remarketing list of website visitors, those are *your* website visitors, and that list can only be used in *your* account, but the list itself, that user data, actually belongs to Google. It's created using Google's platform (Google Analytics or the Google tag) and you have no way to identify the individuals who are actually on that list.

Same with a YouTube remarketing list; it's built based off of your YouTube channel, but YouTube users are *Google's* customers, not your customers, and Google is the only one who actually knows who they are. You can't take a list of YouTube users over to Meta to show ads to them there; you can only use it within Google's platform, via Google Ads.

Contrast this with your customer list. Those are *your* customers, and the list itself sits on *your* computer or *your* CRM. Google knows nothing about your customers until you upload that list. The list itself is not created using Google's platform, so you can absolutely identify the individuals on that list without Google.

This personally identifiable information (PII for short) is seen as the holy grail in marketing because, since it's first-party, you're not reliant on cookies to reach those users.

Google calls remarketing to your customer list Customer Match, as it enables you to *reach your customers on Google's platforms by sharing your first-party data with Google*. You are matching your customer data with Google's customer data - Customer Match.

What you need to know about Customer Match

According to Google, "Customer Match lets you use your online and offline data to reach and re-engage with your customers across Search, the Shopping tab, Gmail, YouTube, and Display."

Translation: Customer Match lets you share your customer data with Google, so that you can find your existing customers via Google Ads, and find new customers like them.

The simplest way to use Customer Match is to upload a file containing your customers' email addresses, but Customer Match can also work with phone numbers, mailing addresses, even names and countries - any key piece of personally-identifiable information (PII). Once this data is in your account, you can use it in lots of different ways, whether you want to show ads to your existing customers, or use your existing customer profiles as the basis for a Lookalike segment. Remember, your customers' data is valuable and precious. Treat it with as much care as you would your most prized possessions. Do NOT upload PII to Google Ads if you do not have user permission to do so. For example, if you purchased a user list from a third-party, do *not* upload it into Google Ads. Not only is it unethical, you'll also risk account suspension for violating Customer Match policies.

Speaking of policies, not all accounts are eligible to use Customer Match. For example, the day you set up a new Google Ads account and launch your first campaign, you will not be able to use Customer Match. See the "account eligibility" section below for more on that.

Once you meet the Customer Match requirements, you can start using your customer list(s) for targeting purposes across all campaign types that allow audience targeting. Both Google and I recommend that you use a customer list as part of your Audience signal for any Performance Max campaigns.

Even if you can't yet target ads to your customer list, you should absolutely still upload it into Google Ads. Smart Bidding and Optimized targeting both use your Customer Match lists as signals for automated bidding and automated targeting, so by just existing in your account, your customer data can help fuel campaign performance.

Additionally, even if you're not spending any money on ads, you can still get audience insights from your customer list. Upload your list via Audience Manager, wait a few days for it to process, and as long as you meet the 1000+ matched user requirement, you can see what Google's audience data shows about your customers: demographics, locations, In-Market segments and Affinity segments.

If you don't see much information in Your data insights, it means that your list isn't large enough for Google to share this information in a privacy-safe way. I've found that customer lists and YouTube lists yield more data than website remarketing lists, probably because Google can more accurately identify these users. I encourage you to check out Tools > Shared Library > Audience Manager > Your data insights to see if you learn anything new about your customers and potentially gain new audience targeting ideas.

I believe that Customer Match is no longer optional in Google Ads, it's table stakes. All accounts in good standing can, and should, use Customer Match. I'll even place it right up there with conversion tracking: don't spend money on ads without it!

As the cookie-less future marches closer and closer, first-party data will be one of the few competitive advantages you have left to drive above-average results with your campaigns. Customer Match or bust, baby. Unless there is a legal or legitimate business reason holding you back, ensure you've got an updated customer list in your Google Ads account *right now*.

Features enabled by Customer Match

Customer Match lets you share your first-party data with Google in a privacy-safe way. In addition to all the great features mentioned above - ad targeting, Smart Bidding, Lookalike creation, audience insights, etc. - there are even more Google Ads features that only become activated once you're leveraging Customer Match.

A newer Google Ads feature that I'm really enjoying testing is conversion-based customer lists. This is the intersection of audience segments and conversion tracking, and you must use Customer Match in order to get access to conversion-based customer lists.

More specifically, when you're using enhanced conversions and Customer Match, Google Ads will automatically create Your data segments of people who have completed your conversion actions. For example, instead of needing to set up a website-based remarketing list of everyone who begins checkout, if you have a conversion action set up for "Begin Checkout," you'll automatically get a segment of users who have begun checkout. Automatically - no effort or updating required! There's a chapter on this later in the book, when we explore "How audiences work with conversion tracking."

Another Customer Match-enabled feature is the new customer acquisition goal. This is an optional setting for Performance Max, Search and Shopping campaigns that directs your campaign to optimize for new customers only. For example, you can set your campaign to *not count a conversion* if it comes from an existing customer, or to *set a different conversion value* if the conversion comes from a new customer.

Personally, I don't use or recommend the new customer acquisition goal very often. A conversion is a conversion, revenue is revenue, and I prefer to use Smart Bidding targets or audience exclusions rather than messing around with conversion data via the new customer acquisition goal. Still, it's yet another newer feature that unlocks for you via Customer Match

Account eligibility

You can upload a customer list to your Google Ads account at any time. As long as your account is in good standing, Google will analyze your list and use it to inform your Smart Bidding and Optimized targeting.

In order to show ads to the customers on your list - to target your list, not just use it for Observation - you must have been spending money on Google Ads for at least 90 days and have a US$50,000 minimum lifetime spend in the account. This is the one that trips up a lot of small businesses, since $50K is a lot of dough! To my knowledge, Google is the only ad platform with a minimum spend requirement to use a customer list. Meta, LinkedIn and others let you use their versions of Customer Match from the get-go. Because of this, I see many smaller businesses opting to use Facebook Ads instead for their customer retargeting campaigns.

List formatting

You can use Customer Match by manually uploading a list to Google Ads, using a third-party platform with a built-in integration, like Salesforce, or connecting your CRM to Google Ads through an automation tool like Zapier. If you're going to upload your list manually, I recommend using Google's template to ensure you've formatted everything correctly.

List size

As with other types of Your data segments, a customer list must have a minimum of 100 active matched records in order to be eligible to show ads on Display and/or to be used as a seed list for a Lookalike segment, and 1000 active matched records in order to be eligible to show ads on Search, YouTube and Gmail.

What does "active matched records" mean? A record is a more accurate way of saying a person or a user, since it's possible that one person might have two different email addresses, and both of them may match to different Google accounts. For example, every day, I use my work profile (thegooglepro@jyll.ca) and my personal Gmail account on my work laptop, my home laptop and my phone. Google

WHAT ARE YOUR AUDIENCE TARGETING OPTIONS IN GOOGLE ADS?

does not know that these two different accounts belong to the same person. In fact, very few companies would be able to connect these two different email addresses to the same person. Since I'm not actually two different people, we call these two separate records.

Your match rate is the percentage of your customer list that Google can identify and associate with signed in Google users. It's unlikely you'll get a match rate of 100%. I typically see match rates in the 70-90% range. You'll see your estimated match rate every time you upload or update your customer list, and the Google Ads interface will display your eligibility to show ads on its various platforms, given this match rate.

But it's not enough to simply match your data with Google's. To meet Google's minimum thresholds, you must have enough matched records belonging to *active users at the time the ad is served*. This is one of those fun little details that, I'll admit, I only learned as I was fact checking this chapter. Some of the records on your customer list will match to Google accounts, but those users won't be currently signed in on Gmail, or Search, etc., because they log out every evening or they recently changed their password or got a new device or a whole host of different reasons. That is why you need a minimum threshold of *active* matched records, not just matched records. That is also why you want to be constantly refreshing your customer lists and populating them with new data, as new records are more likely to be active than older records.

Given the active matched records thresholds and benchmarks, you should plan to have at least 1200-1300 users on your customer list in order to meet the 1000 minimum active match records threshold to start using Customer Match for ad targeting.

Customer Match policies
There are very strict policies you must comply with in order to use Customer Match. For example, you must collect your data directly from users in order to comply with Google's policies. That means no purchasing lead lists from third-party sellers, no email list sharing with complementary businesses, no taking that list of customers from your other business and uploading it to the Google Ads account for this one. The privacy policy on your website must clearly state that you share customer data with third parties (in this case, Google is a third party), and you must obtain consent where required by law.

I am not a lawyer (obviously) so please consult with a lawyer if you have any concerns about using Customer Match, or any other type of remarketing list. You can also check the Customer Match policy page on the Google Ads Help Center for the most up-to-date requirements.

☑ **Remember this! Four types of Your data segments in Google Ads**
Website visitors: people who've visited your website. Enabled by connecting Google Analytics to Google Ads, or by installing the Google tag on your website.
App users: people who've used your app. Enabled by connecting Firebase or a third-party platform to Google Ads.
Google content engagers: people who've interacted with your Google content, like YouTube or Google Search results. Enabled by connecting your YouTube account to Google Ads (YouTube remarketing), or automatically in your account (Engaged audience).
Customer list: people who've given you their email address, phone number or mailing address. Enabled by connecting your CRM to

Google Ads or manually uploading a spreadsheet.

Limitations on Remarketing

The ability to show ads to people your business already knows is a privilege, not a right. This can be a bit counterintuitive. You already "know" these users, so to speak, so why can't you show ads to them? In order to protect users, Google has minimum list size requirements and personalized advertising policies. The list size requirements help maintain user privacy, and the personalized advertising policies ensure that you comply with local laws, and don't inadvertently cause harm.

List size

Your data segments must have at least 100 active matched records in order to use them for audience targeting on the Display network, and at least 1000 active matched records for Google Search, YouTube and Gmail. Since the number of active matched records will be smaller than your total list size, you can check your eligibility for each platform under Tools > Shared Library > Audience Manager > Your data segments. Feel free to edit this report and add columns for Match rate (for Customer Match), Source, Creation date, or whatever else might be useful for you.

Personalized advertising policies

In order to comply with local laws and protect user privacy, there are certain customer segments and industries that are not allowed to use any remarketing features. This is called the Personalized advertising policy, and I highly recommend you consult the Google Ads policies page at https://support.google.com/adspolicy for a comprehensive understanding of how and where you can advertise. It may surprise you to learn that your product or service offering falls within a sensitive or restricted industry.

If you operate in a "sensitive interest category," then you cannot use any Your data segments, Lookalike segments, Audience expansion or Custom segments in Google Ads. Sensitive interest categories include:

- *Legal restrictions*, where ads personalization would be against the law. For example, when users are under 13, or if you're advertising alcohol or gambling
- *Personal hardships*, where ads personalization might exploit users' struggles. For example, health treatments, predatory lending products, divorce services, et al
- *Identity and belief*, where ads personalization might perpetuate discrimination. For example, showing ads based on race, ethnicity, religion, political affiliation, et al
- *Sexual interests*, where ads personalization might expose private behaviour. For example, contraceptives, adult toys, and other things I won't write here as I don't want my book to get flagged for sexual content!
- *Access to opportunities*, where ads personalization might promote unfair biases. For example, real estate listings, job opportunities, credit and loans, et al

Note that you can still use Google's audience segments (more on that in the next chapter), Optimized targeting and Audience signals in a sensitive interest category. You can also use Combined segments, as long as they only include Google's audience segments.

Google's ad policies could be a whole separate book unto

themselves, so I will reiterate that you should check the Google Ads policies page at https://support.google.com/adspolicy if you get an unexpected Status showing up in your Google Ads account, like Eligible (Restricted). The Advertising Policies Help Center offers plenty of helpful troubleshooting tips. When we discuss building your own audience strategies later in this book, I will also share tips and tricks for reaching your ideal audience when you operate in a sensitive interest category.

Cheat Sheet: Your data segments

	Search	Shopping	Display	Video	Demand Gen	PMax
Inclusion	✓	✓	✓	✓	✓	✓
Exclusion	✓	✗	✓	✓	✓	✗

	Combined segments	Custom combination segment	Audience builder	Audience signal
Inclusion	✓	✓	✓	✓
Exclusion	✓	✓	✓	✗

Google's data

It will come as a surprise to NO ONE that Google knows a lot about you, and about billions of internet users around the world.

In fact, I encourage you to check out My Ad Center on Google right now, at https://myadcenter.google.com/customize, to see exactly how Google is personalizing your ads based on your data.

When I look at the brands that Google has recently added to my profile, I see Radio Flyer, Evenflo, Kit and Ace, Veronica Beard, L.L.Bean, Amazon, Lululemon. I've recently been researching stroller wagons (it's a thing!) and new work clothes - from my Chrome browser on my Pixel phone - so of course, Google knows it and is personalizing my ads accordingly.

As an internet user, you may have *feelings* about this. I get it. I'm not here to discuss the ethics or implications of a "free" internet that's paid for by advertising dollars chasing your eyeballs. (Although from the way I phrased that sentence, you can probably deduce my own feelings about it.)

As an advertiser, you LOVE this because it allows you to reach your ideal customer based on *who they are*.

Google Ads offers four categories of audience segments for you to target, based on Google's proprietary data about its billions of global users:

1. **Who they are → Detailed demographics:** going beyond basic demographic information to provide deeper segmentation options based on life and career stages.
2. **What their interests and habits are → Affinity segments:** a compilation of user behaviour into advertiser-friendly "packages." Great for awareness marketing.

3. **What they are actively researching → In-Market segments:** people who are getting ready to purchase specific products or services. A high-intent prospecting audience.
4. **What they are actively planning → Life events:** people who are currently going through a significant life transition, such as graduating, getting married or moving.

Let's explore each one in greater detail, including their capabilities, compatibilities and potential use cases.

Detailed demographics

Detailed demographics in Google Ads allow you to reach people based on who they are. What makes them detailed? Most campaign types allow you to include or exclude users based on their Demographics: their inferred age range, gender, household income range and parental status. Detailed demographics go one step further, providing more - you guessed it - *detail* about those core demographics.

Keep in mind that both Demographics and Detailed Demographics are *inferred* based on user behaviour. While we tell Meta our age and gender when we set up a Facebook profile, and we tell LinkedIn what company we work at when we set up a LinkedIn profile, we don't explicitly tell Google this information since it doesn't own a social network, so we're never filling out a profile on a Google platform.

Instead, Google analyzes our online behaviour to infer (or guess) our gender, age range, job, etc. Some of this will be accurate, and some will be wildly inaccurate.

For example, I just checked My Ad Center for my work profile (thegooglepro@jyll.ca) and Google thinks I am:

- Age: 35-44 (correct)
- Gender: Male (incorrect)
- Relationship status: Not enough information to determine (lol)
- Parenting: Not a parent (incorrect)
- Homeownership: Homeowner (correct)
- Education: Bachelor's Degree (kind of correct, I also have a Master's Degree)
- Industry: Technology (I'll count that as correct)
- Employer size: Small employer (correct)

Now compare that to my personal Gmail account, which I've used for more than a decade across countries, devices and contexts. What does Google think it knows about me over there?

- Age: 35-44 (correct)
- Gender: Female (correct)
- Relationship status: Married (correct)
- Parenting: no data. Now I recall that I turned this off when we were experiencing fertility issues, because I didn't want to see ads about baby products. Yes, you can do that in My Ad Center!
- Homeownership: Homeowner (correct)
- Education: Advanced degree (correct)
- Industry: Technology (correct)
- Employer size: Small employer (correct)

That was a lot better. I'm not sharing these examples to discourage you from using Demographic filters or Detailed demographic audiences, I simply want to demonstrate that none of this stuff is perfect - and in spite of that, you can still use these audiences to drive great results.

Now that I've given you a very personal look at my ads profile, you can start to see where the Detailed demographic audience segments come from. As an advertiser, you can choose to either target or exclude users based on:
- **Parental Status:** for example, Parents of Infants or Parents of Teens
- **Marital Status:** Single, In a Relationship or Married
- **Education:** for example, High School Graduate or Advanced Degree holder
- **Homeownership Status:** Homeowners or Renters
- **Employment - Company Size, Industry:** for example, Healthcare Industry

As you can see, there are about a dozen different Detailed demographic segments you can use in Google Ads in your Search, Shopping, Display, Demand Gen or Video campaigns, as well as your Performance Max Audience signals.

When should you use Detailed demographics? When your offering is only relevant for a certain type of user. For example, if you sell home services that only a homeowner, not a renter, would purchase, excluding "Renters" from your campaign would be a good idea to avoid wasting money targeting users who are unlikely to convert. Notice that I am not recommending targeting "Homeowners," I'm suggesting that you exclude "Renters." There is a third pool of users out there for whom Google doesn't know if they're a homeowner or a renter. By excluding "Renters," rather than only including "Homeowners," I'm ensuring that those *unknowns* are still included in my ad targeting. Many of my potential customers probably have a homeownership status that is unknown to Google, so let's still show them ads. But if Google knows that someone is a renter, then we can safely exclude them.

Think of Detailed demographics as a helpful narrowing mechanism to focus your advertising efforts. I usually see B2B advertisers make more use of Detailed demographics than B2C advertisers, specifically the "Company Size" and "Industry" segments.

Remember, Detailed demographics are not the same thing as Demographics. Although you'll find them both in your campaign or ad group under Audiences, keywords & content > Audiences, audience segments (including Detailed demographics) sit separately from Demographics.

Here are my top two tips for you if you are planning to exclude certain Demographics from your campaign:

1. **Don't ignore the Unknown.**

    Many users' age, gender, parental status and household income will be unknown to Google. If your product is only relevant for women, feel free to exclude Men, but keep Women and Unknown included in your campaign. Targeting only Women, not Men nor Unknown, can drive up your costs since you're trying to reach a much smaller group of people, and those people will be in higher demand from advertisers since their Demographics are known.

    I call excluding "Unknown" the nuclear option, because I do resort to it sometimes when campaign performance is really, really wonky. For example, a Video Views campaign that, no matter what I try, continually serves the majority of its Placements on kids content. Or spam leads that

just will not quit, after exhausting all other options. That's the key, though - exhaust all other options. By excluding Unknown, you remove a ton of potential inventory, so your costs will rise significantly. But it could be the thing you need to get your targeting algorithm back on track.
2. **Only adjust Demographics if you really, really need to.**
   If your services could be useful to anyone, don't touch the Demographics. It can be tempting to only target the top 10% of households, for example, but doing so can drive up your costs unnecessarily and cause you to miss out on conversions from other demos. Especially if you're using a Smart Bidding strategy, Google is already considering the demographics of your ideal audience and adjusting your bids accordingly.

Affinity segments

Affinity segments in Google Ads allow you to reach people based on their interests and habits. How does Google know people's interests and habits? Google sees a lot of what we do online: what we search for, what websites we visit, what apps we have on our phones, what videos we watch, etc. Based on those observations, Google has a pretty good idea of who is a "Luxury Shopper" or a "Bargain Hunter," who is a "Snowbound Traveler" or a "Beachbound Traveler" (or both!), and who is a "Metalhead" or a "Rap & Hip Hop Fan" or a "Country Music Fan" or none of the above.

Humans are complex creatures. Some users may be part of dozens of Affinity segments, while others may be part of few or none. Because Affinity segments are based on hobbies and interests, which are relatively stable over time, users tend to be persistently associated with the same segments. This is one of the key features that separates Affinity segments from the more transitory In-Market segments or Life Events segments (we'll get to those next). It also means that if you're running campaigns targeting Affinity segments for a long period of time, you'll probably want to refresh your ad creative more frequently, since you'll be reaching a lot of the same users again and again.

There are about 150 different Affinity segments you can use in your Search, Shopping, Display, Demand Gen or Video campaigns, as well as your Performance Max Audience signals.

When you select an audience to add to your campaign, you can choose the parent category, sub-category, sub-subcategory, etc. Selecting the parent category will include all of its sub-categories, plus other users who may not fit into a sub-category, but do fit the parent. For example, selecting the "Banking & Finance" Affinity segment (parent category) for your campaign will target people who are "Avid Investors" (sub-category) and people who "Bank Online" (sub-category), plus other people who may not invest and may not bank online, but are nonetheless very interested in Banking & Finance. This same logic applies to all kinds of audience segments.

Affinity segments are a great starting point for prospecting campaigns or cold traffic, as they are relatively broad. Because they are so large and broad, I don't recommend using Affinity segments as part of a Performance Max Audience signal.

In-Market segments
In-Market segments in Google Ads allow you to reach people based on what they are actively researching. As I noted a few pages back,

WHAT ARE YOUR AUDIENCE TARGETING OPTIONS IN GOOGLE ADS?

Google knows that I am now in the market for a stroller wagon because I started searching for "stroller wagon reviews" and "wonderfold canada" recently, and I started browsing baby product review sites.

I'm hoping to purchase a stroller wagon before the end of the summer, so by fall, I will no longer be in the market for a stroller wagon. *(Update as I'm editing the book: I did, in fact, purchase a stroller wagon.)* This is one of the key things that differentiates Affinity segments from In-Market segments. People's affinities, their interests and hobbies, are relatively stable over time, whereas people's purchasing needs are constantly changing. This means that the users who make up Google's various Affinity segments don't turn over very frequently, whereas the users who make up Google's various In-Market segments are constantly changing. From an ad creative perspective, you probably don't need to refresh your creative as frequently if you're targeting In-Market segments, since the people in these segments are always changing.

How long do users stay on an In-Market segment, like "Web Hosting" or "Fishing Equipment" or "Minivan & SUV Rental"? Until they're no longer in the market, i.e. until Google has determined that they're no longer displaying online behaviour that matches this segment, either because they've already made their purchase, or they've abandoned their intent to purchase. For big-ticket items like travel or cars or homes, users may be classified as part of the In-Market segment for months or even years. For more impulse or immediate items like "Makeup & Cosmetics" or "Refrigerator Accessories" or "Gift Baskets," users may be classified as part of the In-Market segment for just days.

There are about 800 different In-Market segments you can use in your Search, Shopping, Display, Demand Gen or Video campaigns, as well as your Performance Max Audience signals.

In-Market segments are great for both cold and warm traffic, since you know these users are currently looking to buy in your category. The downside is that once someone is classified as part of an In-Market segment, you may be too late; they may already be deep into the consideration phase with your competitors.

For example, if you sell mattresses, you may be tempted to target the In-Market segment for mattresses. That could be a profitable audience for you, and it's absolutely worth testing. But think about it: how does Google know that someone is currently shopping for a mattress? Because they've searched for mattresses, they've been to mattress stores, they've visited the websites of mattress retailers; they've done all that research activity *in order to* make it onto the "In-Market for Mattresses" audience segment.

If your strategy is just to target that segment, you'll be reaching a lot of potential customers too late; it's like starting the race a full minute after your competitors. This is why I came up with my Non-linear Targeting audience strategy, which we'll explore later in this book when I show you how to build an effective audience strategy.

Life events

Life events in Google Ads allow you to reach people based on what they are actively planning. They work very similarly to In-Market segments, which is why you'll usually find them grouped with In-Market segments under a menu called "What they are actively researching or planning."

The key difference between In-Market segments and Life event segments is simply how the user criteria is framed; In-Market segments are built around specific products or services that *people are looking for*, whereas Life Event segments are based around significant transitions that *people are going through*. There are about a dozen Life events categories you can use in Google Ads. You can use Life events segments in your Display, Demand Gen and Video campaigns, as well as your Performance Max Audience signals. Life events are not compatible with Search or Shopping campaigns. Each Life event category has a "Recently" segment and a "Soon" segment. For example, under the "College Graduation" Life event, you can target a segment called "Recently Graduated," you can target a segment called "Graduating Soon," and/or you can target the entire "College Graduation" segment, which would include both those who have recently graduated and those who are graduating soon.

Life events are a great complement to your audience targeting strategies, and work best when your ad creative appeals to those going through that life change. For example, perhaps you sell credit & lending products. There is an In-Market segment for "Credit & Lending," with a dozen sub-categories for "Credit Cards," "Student Loans," etc. A complementary approach would be to target the Life Events "Purchasing a Home Soon" or "Recently Married" or "Renovating a Home Soon" to reach people who will likely need credit & lending products, and show them ads that demonstrate how your products can help them through the life change they're experiencing.

☐ Remember this! Four types of audience segments based on Google's data

Detailed demographics: who they are; deeper demographics based on life and career.
- Examples: Parents of Toddlers, Works in the Construction Industry

Affinity segments: what their consistent interests and habits are.
- Examples: Beauty Mavens, Frequently Dines Out

In-Market segments: what they're actively researching and getting ready to buy.
- Examples: In-Market for Trips to Paris, In-Market for Shoes

Life events: what they're actively planning around a significant life transition.
- Examples: Recently Graduated, Getting Married Soon

Cheat Sheet: Google's data

	Search	Shopping	Display	Video	Demand Gen	PMax
Detailed demographics	✓	✓	✓	✓	✓	✓
Affinity segments	✓	✓	✓	✓	✓	✓
In-Market segments	✓	✓	✓	✓	✓	✓
Life events	X	X	✓	✓	✓	✓

	Combined segments	Custom combination segment	Audience builder	Audience signal
Detailed demographics	✓	X	✓	✓
Affinity segments	✓	X	✓	✓
In-Market segments	✓	X	✓	✓
Life events	✓	X	✓	✓

A combination of your data and Google's data

We've gone through all the different ways you can share your business data with Google to re-engage users. You might call this remarketing or retargeting, and Google calls it Your data segments.

We've also covered all of the pre-built Google audiences. These segments take Google's insights about billions of people's behaviour and package it up so that you, as an advertiser, can just pick them off the shelf. Give me the people who just got a new pet, please!

In my experience, most beginner and intermediate Google Ads users stop their audience usage right here. They set up some remarketing, dabble in Google's audiences and call it a day.

That's cool. But it's also missing the *magic* of audiences.

Google offers a third kind of unique audience targeting: combining your data with Google's data to create Custom segments and Combined segments. This is where the real power in audience targeting comes in, and it's the Google Ads feature that got me excited to write this book in the first place.

And if there's one thing I love even more than audience targeting, it's a Venn diagram to visualize audience targeting:

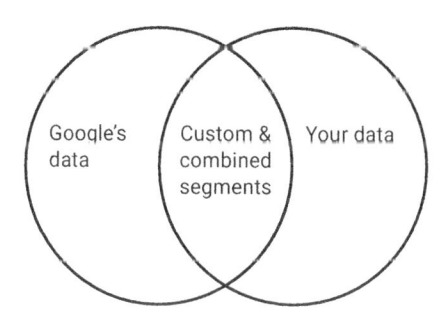

Custom segments

Custom segments let you take additional pieces of information that Google knows about people, and slice and dice it in a way that's uniquely valuable to your business. With Custom segments, you can show ads to users who have certain online behaviours that you find particularly intent-rich.

More specifically, Custom segments give you four inputs for creating your own unique audience segments. In Google Ads, you can create a Custom segment based on:

- People with certain **interests or purchase intentions**
- People who **searched for certain terms**
- People who **browse types of websites**
- People who **use types of apps**

For simplicity, we'll call these four inputs "interests," "searches," "websites," and "apps."

Custom segments are not only a hybrid of your data and Google's data, they are also a hybrid of audience targeting and content targeting. With a Custom segment, you are building an *audience* based on the *types of content* people have engaged with.

You are turning content targeting into audience targeting.

Did I just blow your mind? Well hold on to your hat, because we're going to take that a step further.

The three types of content targeting in Google Ads are Topics, Placements and Keywords.

Topics-based content targeting lets you show ads to people *as they are engaging* with content about certain topics. **Interest-based** Custom segments let you show ads to people who *have engaged with content about* certain topics.

Placements-based content targeting lets you show ads to people *as they are using* certain websites and apps. **Website-based** and **app-based** Custom segments let you show ads to people *who have used* certain types of websites and apps.

Keyword-based content targeting (in a Search campaign) lets you show ads to people *when they are searching* for certain terms. **Searches-based** Custom segments let you show ads to people *who have searched for* certain terms.

Pretty cool, right?

Let's look at a practical example of how you can take an audience-based approach or a content-based approach to reach similar users and achieve similar objectives.

Example: You want to reach people who are in the market for Google Ads training.

- Option 1: Launch a **Search campaign**, with keywords like "google ads course" and "learn google ads"
- Option 2: Launch a **Demand Gen campaign**, with a Custom segment based on people who recently searched for terms like "google ads course" and "learn google ads"

In this example, both options will help you reach people who are currently in the market for Google Ads training. People are searching for "google ads course" and "learn google ads," and you can either show an ad to them *at the moment they're searching* by using *keywords* in a *Search* campaign (content targeting) or you can show an ad to them later *as they're doing other things online* by using a *Custom segment* in a *Demand Gen* campaign (audience targeting).

While there are a variety of reasons to pursue one strategy or the other (or both), it usually comes down to cost. Search clicks are expensive! For keywords like this, in the United States, I'd expect to pay at least $20 per click. In a Demand Gen campaign targeting Custom segments, I'd expect to pay more like $1 to $2 per click. The Search clicks would likely convert better, but 10x better than Demand Gen? The only way to know would be to test, test, test.

We'll go through plenty more examples throughout this book, and explore when to use a content-based strategy, an audience-based strategy, or both. But first, we need to understand how Custom segments can be built, and ensure we don't confuse an audience segment *based on content engagement* with actual content targeting itself.

How to use Custom segments

Custom segments are compatible with Display and Demand Gen campaigns. Custom segments are not compatible with Search or Shopping campaigns.

For Video and Performance Max campaigns, you can use something called a Custom interest, which is similar to but subtly different from Custom segments. It's also quite new. I'll explain Custom interests in more detail in a few pages.

You can target your ads with Custom segments, but you can't use Custom segments as exclusions.

You can create Custom segments within a campaign or ad group, or in Audience Manager. Whichever way you choose, the Custom segments you create will be available for all campaigns in the account to use. For example, if you create a Custom segment while setting up a Display campaign, you can see and edit this segment later by going to Tools > Shared Library > Audience Manager > Custom segments. If you edit the Custom segment, those changes will be applied everywhere that segment is in use.

When you create a new Custom segment, the default is to create it based on interests. If you would like to add searches, you'll need to change your selection from interests to searches (you can't have both in the same segment). If you would like to add websites or apps, you'll need to expand those options, then type your inputs.

What's the difference between interests and searches in a Custom segment, and why can you only choose one? When you input interests, Google will build an audience of people who've displayed those interests or purchase intentions, and you can target them with ads from a Display or Demand Gen campaign. That one's straightforward.

When you input searches, things work a little differently. Google will build an audience of people who've searched for those things on Google, YouTube or other Google-owned properties, and you'll be able to show ads to those users *only on Google-owned properties*.

As a reminder, the main Google-owned properties (for Google Ads purposes) are Google search, Google Maps, YouTube, Gmail, and Discover. That means that if you create a Custom segment based on searches and add it to a Display campaign, your Custom segment will not work as intended. Display ads primarily show on non-Google-owned properties (millions of websites and apps on the Display network), and non-Google owned properties are *not compatible* with searches-based Custom segments. In this scenario, Google would treat your searches inputs as if they were interests inputs - without telling you.

If you create a Custom segment based on searches, and you want to target those users, you must add it to a Demand Gen campaign. This campaign type primarily serves on Google-owned properties (YouTube,

Gmail, Discover) so your searches-based Custom segment will work as intended: showing ads to people who've searched for certain terms on Google search, YouTube, etc.

Note that in a Demand Gen campaign, you have the option to include Video partners inventory. Video partners are websites other than YouTube that play videos and have video ad inventory. Just like publishers can monetize ad space on their websites using AdSense, Video partners can monetize ad space in their video players using AdSense or similar Google platforms. Honestly, I'm still shocked that Demand Gen campaigns have the option for Video partner inventory, because it means that Demand Gen campaigns no longer *only* serve on Google-owned properties. If you include Video partners in your Demand Gen campaign, then just as with Display, Custom segments with *searches* inputs will be treated as Custom segments with *interests* inputs, when serving on Video partner inventory.

Deep breath, you've got this!

You can add up to three inputs within the same Custom segment: searches or interests (not both), websites, apps. When you select multiple types of inputs within a Custom segment, Google treats that as an OR relationship. This means that in order for a user to match your segment, they must have:

	searches or interests that match your terms
OR	browsed those types of websites
OR	used those types of apps

If you would like to narrow your segment - for example, to only show ads to people who visit certain types of websites AND use certain types of apps - you'll need to create multiple Custom segments, then put them together in a Combined segment (we'll get to those next).

As you're building your Custom segment, you can see the estimated size and demographics of the audience you're creating in the Segment insights, on the right-hand side of your screen. This can help you gut check whether or not your Custom segment is likely to reach your intended audience.

To use this feature, build your segment inputs first, i.e. type in your interests/searches, websites or apps. Then, before you Save, expand the Segment Insights and customize the country and language settings to those you intend to use for your campaign. Google will show you the:

- Estimated range of available weekly impressions. Remember, this is not unique reach or market size, it is impressions: the number of times your ads could potentially be seen in a week. The same person could potentially see your ads many times.
- Estimated gender split
- Estimated age range split
- Estimated parental status split

Due to privacy regulations and Google's personalized advertising policies, you may not be able to add certain interests, searches, websites or apps to your Custom segment. For example, If you try to advertise to people who've recently searched for adult toys, your Custom segment will either not let you Save, or will Save but will not serve ads. You may see a yellow warning above your Segment insights that says "This keyword is not included in the segment insights estimate." If so, simply remove that input before saving your Custom segment.

For more details on Google's personalized advertising policies, go back to the remarketing chapter - most policies that apply to remarketing also apply to Custom segments. For advice on how to use audience targeting in a sensitive category, I've got a chapter on that later in the book, in the section about how to build an effective audience strategy.

Custom interests, Custom search terms and Search themes

Custom segments are complicated. Recent Google Ads product changes make this fabulous audience targeting feature even more complicated. To the keen-eyed observer, it's clear that Custom segments are going through a transition.

Recently, Google changed how Custom segments work and created three "offspring" with similar capabilities: Custom interests, Custom search terms and Search themes. These offspring were incubated, if you will, under the behemoth that is Performance Max campaigns. We'll be discussing Performance Max and all its audience targeting idiosyncrasies later. For now, stick with me as we explore some Google Ads history. By reviewing the past, we'll better understand where we've landed right now, and where Custom segments are likely going in an increasingly automated future.

When Performance Max campaigns first launched, you could add Custom segments to your Performance Max Audience signals. In fact, Google encouraged this as a best practice, and I agreed with that. I created Custom segments and added them to every Audience signal I encountered.

Well, you can't use Custom segments with Performance Max anymore, nor can you use them with most Video campaigns, but you *can* use something very similar called Custom interests.

A Custom interest is the same as a Custom segment except it

does not let you include searches. A Custom interest can be built based on users who've expressed certain interests or purchase intentions, visited certain types of websites or used certain types of apps.

Interests or searches, websites, and apps = Custom segments.

Interests, websites, and apps, but no searches = Custom interests.

Don't worry - I've got a cheat sheet for you at the end of this section, and it's also available for you to download from my *Inside Google Ads* course.

Let's unfold the next layer.

For Performance Max, Google made this change around the same time it added Search themes as an "automation guiding tool" in Performance Max. According to Google, Search themes "allow you to provide Google AI with valuable information about what your customers are searching for and which topics lead to conversions for your business." Sounds kind of like the *searches* part of a Custom segment, right?

Whenever we are "providing AI with information," that's code for "you can tell us what you want, but ultimately, we'll do whatever we want to do." When we get to Optimized targeting and Audience signals in the section on automated targeting, that code will become commonplace for understanding how Google Ads targeting is evolving: more "signals," less "targeting."

For Video campaigns, this change from Custom segments to Custom interests is even more recent - as in, it's occurring right now as I'm writing this book. You can no longer use Custom segments in Video campaigns that use the Video views, Efficient reach, Target frequency, Non-skippable reach or Audio subtype. However, you can use Custom interests, and you can also use something called Custom search terms.

(Note: while Custom segments are still an option in the Drive conversions and Ad sequence Video campaign subtypes, conversion-focused Video campaigns are being upgraded to Demand Gen, and Ad sequence is a funky subtype that will likely be brought in line with the other remaining Video campaign subtypes soon. For simplicity, from this point forward, we'll assume Custom segments are 100% gone from Video campaigns.)

Although Custom search terms and Search themes have different names, they are essentially the same as a Custom segment based on searches. You are creating an *audience* based on *things people have searched for*. You are turning content targeting (searches) into audience targeting (people who have searched). Remember, though, that Custom search terms function as actual ad targeting, just as Custom segments did in Video campaigns. However, Search themes only function as signals, just as Custom segments did in Performance Max campaigns.

By using Custom search terms in a Video campaign, you can show ads to people who searched for your inputs. That audience will work as intended on YouTube only, since YouTube is a Video campaign's only Google-owned inventory. If you have Video partners enabled, then your ads will show there to people whose *interests or purchase intentions* match your search terms.

By using Search themes in a Performance Max campaign, you're providing a signal for the automation about the kinds of users you're looking to reach, based on things they've searched for.

While there are a few more differences, we have enough framing now to understand that even though we can't use Custom segments in Performance Max or Video campaigns anymore, we still have the same *capabilities* under different names: Custom interests, Custom search terms and Search themes.

WHAT ARE YOUR AUDIENCE TARGETING OPTIONS IN GOOGLE ADS?

You may have come across some additional terminology in your Google Ads training like Custom affinity, Custom intent and Custom audiences. These are older concepts in Google Ads that pre-date Custom segments.

- Custom affinities allowed you to build an audience segment based on people's interests.
  - Sound familiar? This is now "interests" in a Custom segment or Custom interest
- Custom intent allowed you to build an audience segment based on things people searched for and websites they visited.
  - Sound really familiar? This is now "searches" and "websites" in a Custom segment. Or, Custom search terms and "websites" in a Custom interest
- Both were upgraded into a new option, Custom audiences, which let you create an audience segment based on things people searched for, websites they visited and apps they used.
  - Sound really, really familiar? This is now Custom segments. Or, Custom search terms and Custom interests.

For a time, you could also add an input to Custom audiences for types of places people visited in the real world, but that was killed pretty quickly - likely due to privacy concerns. It was fun while it lasted!

When Google rebranded "audiences" to "segments," Custom audiences became Custom segments, and they lived happily ever after...

Just kidding. As we now know, Custom segments got split into Custom interests and Search themes for Performance Max, and Custom interests and Custom search terms for Video campaigns.

Ready for that cheat sheet now?

Musings & Predictions for Custom segments
Given the way this cookie usually crumbles, I'm sure more changes to Custom segments are coming for Display and Demand Gen, too. I'll even go one step further and predict that by 2026, Custom segments will be relegated to Google Ads history. I mean, "upgraded" to Custom interests and Custom search terms, and I'm sure some other confusing names that Google's product managers are brainstorming with Gemini right now. *(Insert mild sarcasm here)*

I also predict that Custom search terms and Search themes show us the audience-based and signal-based future of search. You pick the types of things your target audience might search for, you guide the automation, but ultimately, Google will use your first-party audience data and conversion data to predict who it should show your ads to next. And then it will show ads to them, regardless of your "signal."

As I'm predicting that Search themes are the future of keywords, I can't help but laugh at how we seem to have come full circle. Smart campaigns, the "Google Ads for Dummies" campaign type, have finally been deprecated, and with them we say goodbye to Keyword themes: words or phrases that help match your ads with Google searches. In a Smart campaign, a single Keyword theme could match to multiple words or phrases, kind of like how a single Search theme can guide your Performance Max campaign towards the kinds of user searches you'd like to advertise on. Hmm, maybe Smart campaigns aren't really gone after all...

One of the truisms of Google Ads is that change is the only constant. The evolution of Custom segments is just one example of that, as is the evolution of keyword matching. But another Google Ads truism we see illustrated here is that everything old is new again. Custom search terms may be a new feature with a new name, with new rules and tricks to get used to, but the core functionality - showing ads to people who've searched for certain things - is not new at all. Custom intent, Custom audiences, Custom segments, Custom search terms, and I'm sure within a few years there will be more "deprecations," "upgrades" and "feature announcements."

This is why I don't view machine learning and automation as an obstacle we must overcome. The core concepts of Google Ads become even more important in an increasingly automated world, not less relevant. Ad rank. Compelling creative. Conversion tracking. Goal-based bidding. Matching user intent. While the individual Google Ads products and features and names may constantly change, the foundation remains remarkably unchanged.

With this mindset, AI becomes a tool to empower us and accelerate growth and open new possibilities, not an existential threat. I've said it before and I'll say it again: work with the system, not against the system, to drive sustainable results.

Tips for success with Custom segments

I may have just predicted the demise of Custom segments, but for now, they are still a powerful tool for Display and Demand Gen campaigns. The 5 tips I'm about to share with you can also apply to Custom Interests, Custom search terms and Search themes for your Video and Performance Max campaigns.

1. Segmentation or consolidation

When creating a Custom segment that uses multiple types of inputs (searches/interests, websites and apps), I recommend splitting each input type into its own Custom segment (or Custom interest) rather than adding them all within one segment.

Why? Adding more options to the Custom segment reduces transparency about what's actually driving good results. For example, maybe the people who've visited certain types of websites are a great fit for my offer and converting well, but the people who use certain types of apps aren't actually a good audience for me, and aren't converting well. If I had it all in one Custom segment, I may determine that the audience isn't working and stop targeting it altogether. By having two separate Custom segments, I can see this performance data in my campaign and adjust accordingly - by pausing the app-based segment and keeping the website-based segment.

Don't: Create a Custom segment with searches (nike, adidas, puma, new balance, lululemon, skechers) and websites (nike.com, adidas.com, puma.com, newbalance.com, lululemon.com, skechers.com) and apps (Nike, Nike Run Club, Nike Training Club, Adidas, Adidas Running, Puma, Lululemon, Fitbit, Map My Run)

Do: Create 3 Custom segments and add all three to your campaign or ad group targeting.

Custom segment with searches (nike, adidas, puma, new balance, lululemon, skechers)

Custom segment with websites (nike.com, adidas.com, puma.com, newbalance.com, lululemon.com, skechers.com)

Custom segment with apps (Nike, Nike Run Club, Nike Training Club, Adidas, Adidas Running, Puma, Lululemon, Fitbit, Map My Run)

2. How many inputs

When you're building a Custom segment (or Custom interest or Custom search terms), I recommend giving it at least 5 options per input, and preferably more like 10-20, to ensure there's enough data to properly build your audience.

Let's illustrate with a popular example: competitor targeting. If you want to target your competitor's customers, it can be tempting to create a Custom segment just based on your competitor's website or app. Remember, though, that Custom segments (and Custom interests) target "the types of people who use" these websites or apps, not necessarily the users of the exact websites or exact apps you choose. If you only provide 1 website, Google isn't going to have a good idea of the type of user you're trying to reach, since any 1 website likely has a lot of different kinds of users. By providing 10 or so websites instead, you're allowing Google to triangulate what kind of user you're looking for, since it can analyze the types of people who would use some or all of those 10 websites and what those users have in common with each other.

Don't: Add only nike.com to your Custom segment

Do: Add nike.com, adidas.com, puma.com, newbalance.com, lululemon.com, skechers.com to your Custom segment

3. Custom segments are a great alternative to search conquesting

Speaking of competitors, Custom segments (and Custom search terms and Search themes) are perfect for competitor targeting. Advertising *when a user searches* for your competitor's brand name can get expensive, but showing ads to *users who've searched for* your competitor is usually quite affordable.

Why is Search conquesting expensive? It's not because Google tries to penalize or discourage this behaviour, it's because of how the ad auction works. As per Google Ads policy, you can't use someone else's trademark in your ad text. This means that Nike can't say

"Adidas" anywhere in the text of its ads. You can, however, use whatever words or trademarks you'd like as keywords. This means that Nike can use the keyword "adidas" and become eligible to show ads when people are searching for Adidas - Nike just can't say "Adidas" in those ads. Because of this, these ads will have low Ad relevance and low Expected click-through rate, which almost certainly means a low Quality Score. This will drag down Nike's Ad Rank for the "adidas" keyword, and in order to compensate for that and remain eligible to show an ad, Nike will need to bid more. A lot more. That's why Search conquesting gets so expensive: Ad Rank fundamentals.

When we use Custom segments or Custom search terms instead, Ad Rank and Quality Score are *not an issue* since the user is not actively searching at the moment we're showing them an ad. Advertising to a competitor-based Custom segment should cost a similar amount to advertising to any prospecting audience.

To use Custom segments as an alternative to search conquesting, simply input your competitors' names as "things people searched for." Then, apply this audience to a Demand Gen campaign. Remember, the "searches" input only works for ads shown on Google-owned properties, so this wouldn't work as intended in a Display campaign, and it wouldn't work as intended in Video partner inventory from a Demand Gen campaign (you can turn Video partners on or off in your campaign settings).

To achieve a similar effect with a Video campaign, add your competitor names as Custom search terms. In a Performance Max campaign, add them as Search themes.

Don't: Use a Custom segment based on searches in a Display campaign

Do: Use a Custom segment based on searches in a Demand Gen campaign, with Video partners turned off

4. How to get search term ideas

Not sure what searches to use in your Custom segment, Custom search terms or Search themes? Look at the top search terms from your Search and/or Shopping campaigns and use them as your starting point. This gives you more opportunities to reach people when they may not be actively searching, but are definitely interested in what you offer.

5. A Custom segment with websites is not the same thing as website placements

Remember, a Custom segment or Custom interest based on websites people have visited is *not the same thing* as placing your ad on those websites.

When you add a Custom segment to the audience targeting of your Display or Demand Gen campaign, or a Custom interest to your Video campaign, you will show ads to people who have visited websites similar to those you've selected. For example, a Custom segment of people who've visited websites like nytimes.com, washingtonpost.com, theguardian.com, cnn.com, bbc.com, economist.com, latimes.com and npr.org will show ads to people who are interested in current events. Those users will see these ads as they are doing other things online, like watching YouTube videos or playing a game. *It will not place your ads on those websites.*

To place your ads on specific websites or apps, you'll need to use content targeting. Specifically, you would need to run a Display or Video campaign and add those websites as Placements.

This is the difference between audience targeting (Custom segments) and content targeting (Placements). You can use both strategies to achieve similar goals, and figure out what works best for your business.

Also remember that a Custom segment or Custom interest based on websites or apps targets users who visit websites *similar to* the ones you've selected, or who use apps *similar to* the ones you've selected. *It does not guarantee that you will reach the exact users of those websites or apps.*

To reach the exact users of those websites or apps, you would need to add them as Placements in a Display or Video campaign. You can only do that if those websites are part of the Google Display Network. The Display Network reaches more than 90% of Internet users worldwide, with 3 million websites and apps included (according to Google), but there are millions more websites and apps that are *not* part of the Display Network.

Don't: I want to show ads to everyone who has used the Nike app (Only Nike can do that, by leveraging their own app-based remarketing)

Do: I want to show ads to the types of people who use apps like Nike, Adidas, Puma, Peloton, Strava, Nike Run Club, Nike Training Club, adidas Running, etc.

☑ **Remember this! Four ways to build a Custom segment**
Interests: People's interests or purchase intentions
Searches: The things people have been searching for
Websites: The types of websites people browse
Apps: The types of apps people use

Custom interests work the same as Custom segments, without the "searches" input. Instead, you can use Custom search terms for Video campaigns and Search themes for Performance Max Audience signals.

Combined segments

By now you've realized that there are a million different ways to reach potential customers with Google Ads audiences. If you thought Custom segments were cool, wait until you hear about Combined segments.

Combined segments let you create an audience that matches multiple targeting requirements. If you've ever heard of audience stacking or audience layering, Combined segments are where that happens in Google Ads.

By using the modifiers AND, OR & NOT, you can weave different Google audiences, remarketing lists and Custom segments together to create highly unique, highly targeted segments. The best way to remember the difference between AND and OR in a Combined segment is that using AND will *narrow* the size of your audience, whereas using OR will *expand* the size of your audience.

If you're a Meta Ads practitioner, creating Combined segments will feel similar to the Detailed targeting you're used to. Or rather, used to be used to. Google Ads isn't the only platform that's constantly changing!

Let's look at an example of Combined segments in action. What if you want to reach parentpreneurs: people who are new parents and new business owners, but not yet current customers?

Here's one way you could build a "Parentpreneurs" audience using Combined segments:

    Life event: Recently Started a Business
    AND
             In-Market: Infant & Toddler Feeding
    OR   Detailed demographics: Parents of Babies
    OR   Detailed demographics: Parents of Toddlers
    NOT   Your data segments: Customer list

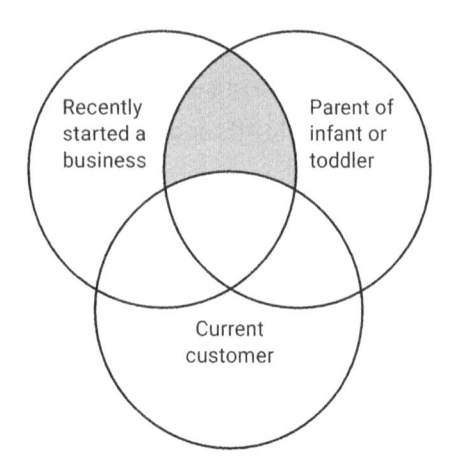

Why not just add all of these audiences to your ad group and call it a day? When you add multiple audiences to a campaign or ad group, Google treats your audience segments as having an OR relationship. Using our parentpreneur example, let's say that you did add these four audiences to your ad group in a Display campaign:

Life event: Recently Started a Business
In-Market: Infant & Toddler Feeding
Detailed demographics: Parents of Babies
Detailed demographics: Parents of Toddlers

This would work identically to creating a Combined segment like this, and adding it to your campaign:

	Life event: Recently Started a Business
OR	In-Market: Infant & Toddler Feeding
OR	Detailed demographics: Parents of Babies
OR	Detailed demographics: Parents of Toddlers

This tells Google that you want to reach people who recently started a business OR people in the market for infant and toddler feeding supplies OR parents of babies OR parents of toddlers. What will happen is that you'll potentially reach a bunch of people who recently started a business, but are *not* parents of infants and toddlers. You'll also potentially reach a bunch of people who are parents of infants and toddlers, but are *not* entrepreneurs.

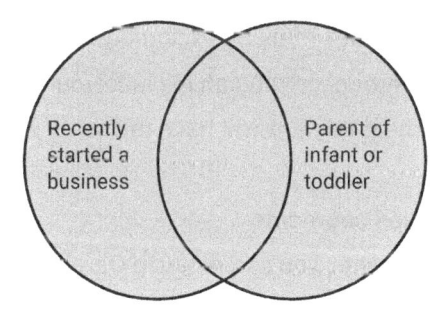

There's nothing wrong with this audience, but it's not going to effectively reach the intersection we want it to reach: parentpreneurs. The universe of people who are both entrepreneurs AND parents is much smaller than the universe of people who are entrepreneurs OR parents. Most of your impressions, clicks and budget will likely get sucked up by the parents and the entrepreneurs before your campaign has a chance to reach those niche parentpreneurs. By creating a Combined segment, we can focus our budget exclusively on reaching that niche.

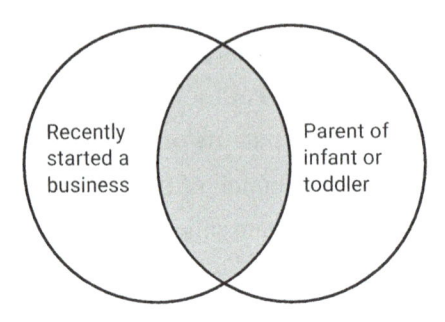

```
          _____
         /     |     \
        /      |      \
       / Recently|Parent of\
      |started a|infant or|
       \business|toddler /
        \      |      /
         \_____|_____/
```

And what about excluding your current customers from seeing these ads? You can achieve this by excluding your customer list from the campaign or ad group, or you can exclude your customer list from the Combined segment itself. It will have the same effect either way.

How to use Combined segments
As with Custom segments, you can create a Combined segment within a campaign or ad group, or from Audience Manager. You can view all the Combined segments in your account by going to Tools > Shared Library > Audience Manager > Combined segments.

Combined segments let you build your audience based on:
- **Google's data:** Detailed demographics, Affinity segments, In-Market segments, Life Events
- **Your data segments:** Website visitors, YouTube segments, Customer list, App users, Engaged audience
- **Custom segments** and Custom interests

Google's data and Your data segments can be layered with AND, OR & NOT logic when building a Combined segment, but Custom segments and Custom interests can only be layered with AND or OR. Just as you can't use Custom segments (or Custom interests) as exclusions in your campaigns or ad groups, you can't use Custom segments (or Custom interests) to exclude people from your Combined segment.

Combined segments are only compatible with Display and Search campaigns. You can target your ads with Combined segments, but you can't use Combined segments as exclusions.

Combined segments are not compatible with Video campaigns (except for the Ad sequence subtype), Demand Gen or Shopping, and they can't be used in Performance Max Audience signals.

You can add multiple Combined segments to a campaign or ad group. Just try not to go overboard and overcomplicate things with dozens of them. As tempting as it can be to try to get super narrow, you are more likely to make your audience too small to serve than to achieve a perfect, super-niche audience.

Also, if you are using multiple Combined segments in your account, make sure you give them very descriptive names so you can easily recall what they're targeting. Future you will be very grateful!

As you're building your Combined segment, you can see the estimated size of the audience you're creating in the Segment estimate settings, on the right-hand side of your screen. This can help you gut check whether or not your Combined segment is likely to reach your intended audience. To use this feature, build your segment inputs first. Then, before you Save, expand the Segment estimate settings and customize to the country and language settings you intend to use for your campaign. Google will show you the Estimated segment size, in the form of estimated weekly impressions. Remember, this is not unique reach or market size, it's impressions; the number of times your ads could potentially be seen in a week.

Combined segments vs. Custom combination segments
A Combined segment is not the only Google Ads feature that lets you stack audiences. There is a similar but different feature called a Custom combination segment.

I've been working in Google Ads for more than a decade and never came across Custom combination segments until a few months ago. When I looked into what they were, I thought it was a joke! And yet here we are.

A Custom combination segment is like a Combined segment, but it only works with inputs from Your data segments. In fact, you'll find it under "Your data segments" in Audience Manager, not under "Combined segments."

For example, if you want to reach people who are either on your email newsletter list or YouTube subscribers, but haven't visited your website in the last 30 days, you could create a Custom combination segment like this:

	Customer list: Newsletter subscribers
OR	YouTube users: YouTube subscribers
NOT	Website visitors: All Users (30 days)

Alternatively, you could do the exact same thing with a Combined segment, creating it like this:

	Customer list: Newsletter subscribers
OR	YouTube users: YouTube subscribers
NOT	Website visitors: All Users (30 days)

While we're talking about feature redundancy in Google Ads, it's worth noting that you can do the exact same thing once more with Audience

WHAT ARE YOUR AUDIENCE TARGETING OPTIONS IN GOOGLE ADS?

Builder, like this:

                Customer list: Newsletter subscribers
OR   YouTube users: YouTube subscribers
EXCLUDE   Website visitors: All Users (30 days)

There are three different ways (that I know of) to create this exact audience in Google Ads. There is also a fourth way to reach the exact same users, without creating a new audience at all. Because we're using an OR relationship for this example, you can simply add your email newsletter list and your YouTube user list to your campaign or ad group audience targeting, and your website visitor list to your campaign or ad group audience exclusions. That would look something like this in your audience segments menu:

                Customer list: Newsletter subscribers
                YouTube users: YouTube subscribers

And then in your audience exclusions, add:

                Website visitors: All Users (30 days)

Of the four options for this example, I like the final one best because:

a. It doesn't require the added step of needing to use a Custom combination segment or a Combined segment (or Audience Builder)
b. You'll be able to see how your customer list performs vs. how your YouTube list performs, and make adjustments accordingly. When both are included in a Combined segment (or a Custom combination segment), you'll only be able to see performance data for that segment as a whole,

not its component parts. If you need to use Audience Builder to create an Audience, perhaps because you're in a Demand Gen campaign so you have no other options, then don't worry - you'll also be able to see how your customer list performs vs. how your YouTube list performs.

For a little fun, let's say you want to do the same thing, but with an AND relationship. You want to reach people who are both newsletter subscribers and YouTube subscribers, but haven't visited your website in the last 30 days. Are there still four different ways to do this?

No. There are two, though!

Option 1: Combined segment

	Customer list: Newsletter subscribers
AND	YouTube users: YouTube subscribers
NOT	Website visitors: All Users (30 days)

Option 2: Custom combination segment

	Customer list: Newsletter subscribers
AND	YouTube users: YouTube subscribers
NOT	Website visitors: All Users (30 days)

Audience Builder won't work because you can't force the AND relationship between two audience segments, and you can only use one Audience per ad group. Similarly, adding the audiences to your ad group targeting "as is" won't work, because that creates an OR relationship, not an AND relationship.

Still, I genuinely do not know why Custom combination segments exist when Combined segments can do the exact same things, plus a whole lot more. When you see what I'm predicting for Combined segments, though, perhaps we'll start to appreciate Custom combination segments a little bit more.

Audience Builder

Audience Builder, internally known at Google as the "Reimagined Audiences Workflow," allows you to create reusable Audiences across campaigns.

I refer to Audiences that have been created in Audience Builder as Audiences with a capital A, vs. audiences or audience segments, the terms I've been using to refer to this whole genre of targeting rather than one specific feature.

The Audience Builder experience has been rolled out for Demand Gen campaigns and Performance Max asset groups. These make for slightly strange bedfellows, since Demand Gen allows for true audience targeting, while Performance Max only allows for Audience signals. In addition to not functioning the same way, Audiences and Audience signals take slightly different inputs:

If you create or edit an Audience in Audience Builder via Audience Manager, it can include:
- Google's audience segments for inclusion
- Custom segments for inclusion
- Your data segments for inclusion or exclusion
- Demographic exclusions

If you create or edit an Audience signal in Performance Max, it will look the same, except it will show Custom interests instead of Custom segments. Search themes can also be added as an asset group signal in

Performance Max, but they "live" separately from the Audience signal.

If you create or edit an Audience in Audience Builder via a Demand Gen campaign, it can include all of the above features, plus Lookalike segments. In fact, the Lookalike creation flow exists *within* Audience Builder, *within* a Demand Gen campaign. Once you've created a Lookalike segment, it will live within that Audience, and it will be visible under Tools > Shared Library > Audience Manager > Your data segments.

My recommendation: Think of Audience Builder as similar to the "Edit audience segments" section in a campaign or ad group, rather than being similar to a Combined segment. There are three key differences between Combined segments and Audience Builder-created Audiences that make them very different in practice, even if they appear similar on first glance.

First, Combined segments let you narrow your targeting through the use of AND, whereas Audience Builder (and campaign/ad group targeting) only supports the OR relationship. For example, if you want to show ads to people who recently moved into a new rental, you could create a Combined segment like this:

              Life Event: Recently Moved
AND   Detailed demographics: Renters

With Audience Builder, you could only do this:
              Life Event: Recently Moved
OR   Detailed demographics: Renters

which means you would be showing ads to all renters, regardless of whether or not they've recently moved, and all people who have recently moved, regardless of whether they own or rent.

Second, Combined segments allow you to exclude Your data segments and Google's audiences. Audience Builder Audiences only let you exclude Your data segments. To reach our target audience of people who recently moved into a new rental, you could create a different Combined segment like this:

              Life Event: Recently Moved
NOT   Detailed demographics: Homeowners

This would create a segment of people who recently moved and are not homeowners, so by process of elimination, they would either need to be renters, or people whose homeownership status is unknown to Google.

You can't do this with Audience Builder, since it only lets you exclude remarketing lists.

Finally, you can include multiple audiences (including multiple Combined segments) in your campaign or ad group targeting, but you can only include one Audience per ad group, or one Audience signal per asset group. This isn't as big a deal as the previous two Audience Builder limitations. It might mean that you need to create multiple ad groups or asset groups to achieve your desired audience targeting, but that's an easy fix.

For example, if you want to show ads to our previously mentioned parentpreneurs Combined segment and to our newly created "renters who recently moved" Combined segment, you could target both audience segments in a single Display ad group or observe both audience segments in a single Search ad group. But in a Demand Gen campaign, you can only choose one Audience per ad group. If you want to show ads to two different Audiences, you would need to put them in separate ad groups within your Demand Gen campaign.

Musings & Predictions for Combined segments
Spoiler alert: I think Combined segments are on the chopping block right now. No insider information on that one, I'm just reading the tea leaves on recent product changes.

Tea leaves: Combined segments used to be compatible with Video campaigns and Discovery campaigns (the precursor to Demand Gen campaigns), but they aren't any more. This is such a recent change that when I (re-)started writing this book, you could use Combined segments in Video campaigns, and before I'd finished writing, you couldn't.

I once said on my *Inside Google Ads* podcast that Display ads are like the garbage backwater of Google Ads, and I stand by that statement. Display campaigns are the land that Google Ads product managers forgot. Now that Display campaigns are the only remaining vestige for Combined segments... that's some tea, alright.

More tea leaves: Combined segments aren't compatible with Performance Max nor Audience Builder. With Performance Max, we can see exactly what Google is planning for the future of Google Ads, and Combined segments have been left out of that vision from day one. Similarly, with Audience Builder, Google went through the effort of reimagining the entire audience creation process, and Combined segments were completely left out of that process.

Even more tea leaves: Custom segments and Combined segments have always gone hand-in-hand as the special place where you can put your data and Google's data together, and create the most niche audiences possible. Given what we already saw is happening to Custom segments, and my prediction that Custom segments as we know them will be gone by 2026, I am sadly starting the doomsday clock for Combined segments, too. I predict that Combined segments will be fully deprecated in Google Ads by 2026.

Why? Super-detailed niche targeting is no longer en vogue on any ad platform. Just as Meta Ads encourages you to "go broad" and has been removing detailed targeting features, Google Ads also wants you to "go broad" and let the machine learning algorithms figure out the right targeting for you. "Going broad" on Google means Performance Max campaigns and Broad Match keywords in Search campaigns - the so-called "Power Pair" (Google's language, not mine).

But why? This one's also not such a mystery. Between Apple's iOS14 update that decimated all ad platforms' data about their iPhone users, the degradation of third-party cookies (even if Chrome isn't deprecating them - yet), changing privacy regulations, anti-trust lawsuits, eroding public trust in tech companies... There are strong technology trends, industry trends and consumer trends running *against* the use of highly personalized, highly targeted digital advertising. Leveraging fully-automated audience targeting allows you to let Google give its best possible shot of finding the best users for your business.

I'm a measured optimist. But I will acknowledge that there are pessimists out there who believe the main motivation is money. The more you leverage automation, like Smart Bidding and fully automated targeting, the more Google can get you to spend.

That's not wrong, but in my opinion, it's misleading. Of course Google wants you, the advertiser, to spend more money. Google is a for-profit company, with a duty to shareholders to maximize profits. It's not Google's first rodeo, though - if you don't see good business results from your Google Ads investment, then you will not continue to spend money. As a for-profit company, Google is incentivized to ensure that *you make money*, as that is the only way to ensure that *you continue to pay Google* and, therefore, that Google will *continue to make money*.

Are there certain individuals at Google, a company with hundreds of thousands of employees, who don't care about you and just want to make as much money as possible? Yes. That would be the case at any company with that many employees and that many billions of dollars at stake.

What I can tell you, as an ex-Googler, is that the vast majority of Googlers, including your newbie Google reps, *want to help you succeed*. These are smart people with good intentions who want to do a good job, and "doing a good job" means helping you make money, which helps Google make money. The challenge I've observed is that the way many Google sales team members are taught to *help you succeed* may not play out in the real world as the *actual* way you will succeed, especially if you are working with a small budget.

Let's stop my sales rep musings for now as we've gone very far afield from Combined segments. tl,dr - Combined segments are probably going away, for a variety of complex reasons, but while you can still use them, here are my top tips for you.

Tips for success with Combined segments: Audience layering

Audience layering, also called audience stacking, is a little piece of jargon we use when we want to add multiple audiences to our campaigns to narrow the reach and get really specific.

With automated targeting and Audience Builder on the way in, and Combined segments on the way out, audience layering may not be long for this world in Google Ads. Still, it's worth a more detailed run-through of how audience layering works using AND, OR & NOT so you can use Combined segments effectively (while they're still around).

Inclusion: use AND to narrow

You can add 2 or more audiences to your Combined segment (or Custom combination segment) using AND. This means that your target audience must match *all* of the audiences listed. For example:

	In-Market: Web Design & Development
AND	In-Market: SEO & SEM Services

means that in order for your ads to be eligible to serve, the user must be both in the market for website design services and in the market for search marketing services - at least, according to Google's understanding of their online behaviour. If they are in the market for website design services, but have not displayed intent for SEO & SEM services, then they will *not* be eligible to see these ads. This is why we say that AND narrows; it creates a much smaller pool of potential users who are eligible to see your ads, since users must match multiple audience requirements.

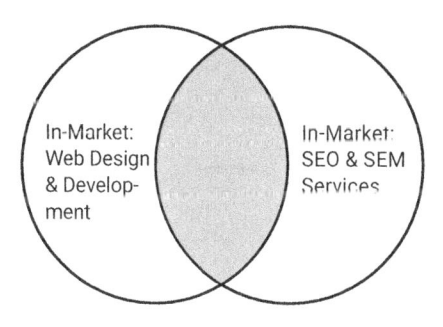

Let's take this one step further and add 3 audiences using AND. In doing so, our target audience must now match all three of the audiences listed. For example:

                In-Market: Web Design & Development
AND   In-Market: SEO & SEM Services
AND   In-Market: CRM Solutions

means that in order for your ads to be eligible to serve, the user must be in the market for website design services, and also in the market for search marketing services, and also in the market for customer relationship management solutions - at least, according to Google's understanding of their online behaviour. If they are in the market for website design services, but have not displayed intent for SEO & SEM services, then they will not be eligible to see these ads. If they are in the market for website design services and search marketing services, but have not displayed intent for CRM solutions, then they still will not be eligible to see these ads. The more audiences you add using AND, the narrower - smaller - your pool of potential users who are eligible to see your ads will get.

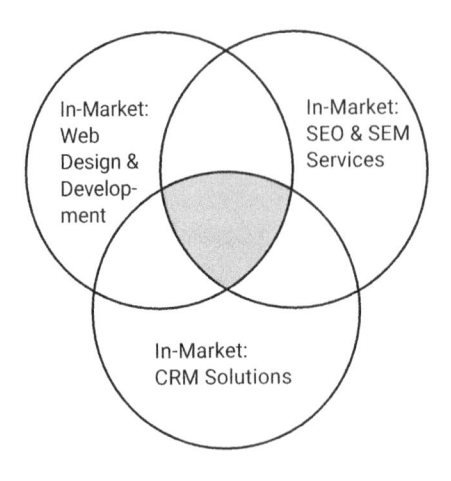

While you can technically stack more audiences using AND, the resulting pool of potential users must be large enough to serve. At a certain point, too many audiences will mean too narrow a pool. If you find yourself needing to stack more than 3 audiences using AND, you might be better served by creating a Custom segment (or Custom interest or Custom search terms) instead.

Inclusion: use OR to expand
You can add 2 or more audiences to your Combined segment (or Custom combination segment) using OR. When you add audiences to your campaign or ad group targeting, or create an Audience in Audience Builder, or create an Audience signal, the audiences you select will have an OR relationship, too. This means that users must only match one of the audiences listed to become eligible to see your ads. For example:

          In-Market: Web Design & Development
OR   In-Market: SEO & SEM Services

means that in order for your ads to be eligible to serve, the user must be in the market for website design services, or in the market for search marketing services - at least, according to Google's understanding of their online behaviour. If they are in the market for website design services, but have not displayed intent for SEO & SEM services, they will still be eligible to see these ads because they match one of the audiences. This is why we say that OR expands; as you add more audiences, it creates a larger pool of potential users who are eligible to see your ads.

[Venn diagram: two overlapping circles labeled "In-Market: Web Design & Development" and "In-Market: SEO & SEM Services"]

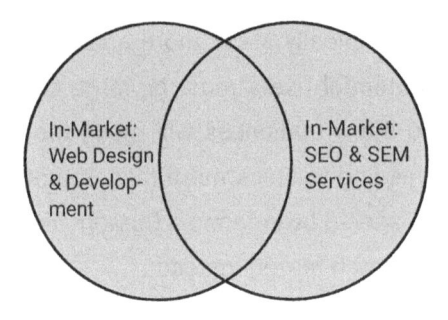

Let's take this one step further and add 3 audiences using OR. Since our target audience must only match one of the three audiences listed, this will make the pool of potential users even larger. For example:

                In-Market: Web Design & Development
OR   In-Market: SEO & SEM Services
OR   In-Market: CRM Solutions

means that in order for your ads to be eligible to serve, the user can be in the market for website design services, or in the market for search marketing services, or in the market for customer relationship management solutions - at least, according to Google's understanding of their online behaviour. There are now 3 potential ways a user can match your audience targeting requirements, instead of just 2. If they are in the market for website design services, but have not displayed intent for SEO & SEM services, then they will still be eligible to see these ads. If they are in the market for website design services and search marketing services, but have not displayed intent for CRM solutions, then they will still be eligible to see these ads. And now, if they are in the market for CRM solutions, but have not displayed any intent for search marketing services or website design services, they will be eligible to see your ads. The more audiences you add using OR, the larger your pool of potential users who are eligible to see your ads will get.

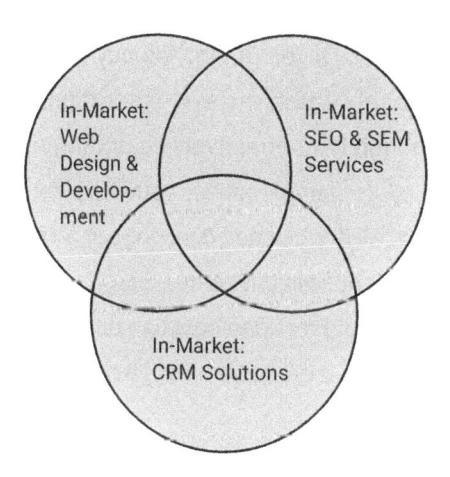

```
        In-Market:           In-Market:
        Web                  SEO & SEM
        Design &             Services
        Develop-
        ment

              In-Market:
              CRM Solutions
```

As you add more audiences using the OR relationship, you may want to consider separate ad groups. Users with different interests, habits or intent will likely need different messaging in order to become enticed to click on your ads. Translation: different ad text / images / video for different audiences.

For example, if you offer both website design services and search marketing services, you might want to have one ad group targeting "In-Market: Web Design & Development," with ad creative that highlights how fabulous you are at growing business' revenue using effectively designed websites. Then, in another ad group, you might want to target "In-Market: SEO & SEM Services," with ad creative that highlights how amazing you are at driving new customer growth using search marketing strategies.

Put yourself in the user's shoes. If I'm looking for help with my website, and I see an ad that says "Best Search Marketers in Canada," that's not going to speak to me. Even an ad that says "Top Digital Marketing Agency" probably won't speak to me either. But "Website Design Made Easy" or "Best Web Development Agency" or "Get a New Website This Week" would surely catch my eye, since that's exactly what I'm looking for, even though I'm not actively searching right now.

Consider your customer personas, your ICP, your target audience, whatever you want to call it, when deciding on your ad group structure, and whether to include audiences in the same ad group, or different ad groups. If that ideal customer would respond best to a different landing page and/or a different ad message, it probably needs a different ad group.

Exclusion: use NOT to narrow

You can add 1 or more audiences to your Combined segments, Custom combination segments, and Audience Builder-made Audiences using NOT. This means that your target audience must *not* match *any* of these excluded audiences. For example:

	In-Market: Web Design & Development
NOT	Your data segments: All Website Visitors (30 days)

means that in order for your ads to be eligible to serve, the user must be in the market for website design services, but must *not* have visited your website in the last 30 days. If they are in the market for website design services, and have visited your website in the last 30 days, they will not be eligible to see these ads.

NOT trumps AND and OR. In other words, if a user matches one of your targeted audiences *and* one of your excluded audiences, they will be excluded. This is why we say that NOT narrows; it creates a smaller pool of potential users who are eligible to see your ads.

Location targeting also works this way. If you target the United States and exclude New York, even though New York is part of the United States, users who are in New York will not be eligible to see your ads. *Exclusion trumps inclusion.*

In a Combined segment, you can exclude any type of audience except a Custom segment (or Custom interest).

In a campaign or ad group, you can exclude any type of audience that you can include for that campaign type. So, if you can include Life Events, you can exclude Life Events. If you can include customer lists, you can exclude customer lists. If you can include Custom combination segments, you can exclude Custom combination segments. The exception is that even if you can include them, you can't exclude Combined segments or Custom segments (or Custom interests).

In an Audience created using Audience Builder, you can only exclude Your data segments. You can include, but not exclude, Google's audiences (In-Market, Affinity, etc.). You cannot include or exclude Combined segments or Custom segments (or Custom interests).

In a Custom combination segment, you can only include or exclude Your data segments. This is why you'll find your Custom combination segments under the Your data segments menu in Audience Manager, in Audience Builder, and in your campaign or ad group audience targeting settings.

☑ **Remember this! Custom vs. Combined segments**

Custom segments allow you to use Google's proprietary user data (about interests, searches, website, and app behaviour) to build audiences that are uniquely meaningful to your business.

In some campaign types, Custom segments have been replaced with **Custom interests**.

Combined segments allow you to layer audiences and reach a more specific, targeted audience. A Combined segment can contain a Custom segment or Custom interest.

Cheat Sheet: Combining your data and Google's data

	Search	Shopping	Display	Video	Demand Gen	PMax
Custom segments	X	X	✓	X	✓	X
Custom interests	X	X	X	✓	X	✓
Custom search terms	X	X	X	✓	X	X
Combined segments	✓	X	✓	X	X	X
Custom combination segments	✓	✓	✓	✓	✓	X

WHAT ARE YOUR AUDIENCE TARGETING OPTIONS IN GOOGLE ADS?

	Combined segments	Custom combination segments	Audience Builder	Audience signal
Custom segments	✓	X	✓	X
Custom interests	✓	X	X	✓
Custom search terms	X	X	X	X
Combined segments	—	X	X	X
Custom combination segments	X	—	✓	X

	Custom segments	Custom interests	Custom search terms	Combined segments	Custom combination segments
Inclusion	✓	✓	✓	✓	✓
Exclusion	X	X	X	X	✓

Automated targeting

We have now discussed all the ways you can choose to reach your ideal customers using audience targeting in Google Ads.

You can reach people who have previously interacted with your business. These "Your data segments" let you reach users who've visited your website, engaged with your Google content, used your app or given you their personally identifiable information.

You can reach people based on Google's proprietary understanding of their online behaviour. These Google audience segments let you reach users based on who they are, what their interests and habits are, what they're actively researching and what they're actively planning.

You can reach people by creating your own segments using Google's data about the content they've engaged with. These Custom segments, Custom interests and Custom search terms let you reach users based on their interests, recent searches, and the types of websites and apps they use.

And you can layer those audiences together with a Combined segment or Custom combination segment to reach a more specific subset or niche of users.

All of these capabilities allow you to tell Google who you're trying to reach. By adding these audience segments to your campaigns, you can then reach the exact types of users you're looking for.

But there's a whole other area of audience targeting that's becoming more and more prevalent, in Google Ads and every other ad platform: automated targeting.

In other words, let the AI figure it out for you.

Why the push towards automated targeting? There are quite a few reasons, but it really boils down to these two:

WHAT ARE YOUR AUDIENCE TARGETING OPTIONS IN GOOGLE ADS?

1. Due to evolving privacy regulations around the world, Google isn't always able to track our online behaviour. That means Google doesn't know as much about us as it used to, which in turn means smaller or less robust audience segments.
2. You may think you know who your ideal customer is, but Google thinks it knows better. By using your conversion data as a guide, Google would rather be given the leeway to go and pick out your best customers for you, rather than being given a specific slice of people and being told to only find conversions within that slice.

Automated targeting takes many names, shapes and forms in Google Ads, and I'm sure that this list will only continue to grow. For now, your automated targeting features in Google Ads are:
1. Optimized targeting
2. Audience expansion
3. Audience signals
4. Search themes
5. Lookalike segments
6. App campaigns (exclusion only)

Let's explore each in detail, including what they all have in common, what sets them apart, and when you can use them.

Optimized targeting

Optimized targeting gives Google permission to show ads to whomever it thinks is most likely to convert, even if those users *do not match* your selected audiences.

I think of Optimized targeting as the Broad Match keyword of the audience world.

Optimized targeting:
- is turned on by default in your campaigns
- will use your landing page, creative assets, audiences and keywords to find ideal users
- will show ads to users who may not match your chosen audience targeting at all

Broad Match keywords:
- are turned on by default in your Search campaigns
- will use your landing page, keywords, and the user's recent search activity to find ideal queries for your ads
- will show ads on searches that may not match the meaning of your keyword at all

The purpose of Optimized targeting is to let the algorithms do what they do best, and find pockets of opportunity to get you a better CPA, ROAS, or whatever metric your bid strategy is optimized for (ergo, *Optimized* targeting).

Put another way, Optimized targeting turns your audience *targeting* into an Audience *signal*.

For example, if you have an ad group that targets the In-market segment "Business Financial Services," Optimized targeting will look at what your converting users have in common, start to build a "converters profile," then go out and show ads to more users who fit that profile. Some or all of them will not be in the market for business financial services, but Google still thinks they are likely to convert.

You can use Optimized targeting in Display and Demand Gen campaigns; in fact, you will be automatically opted in to Optimized targeting unless you turn it off. (Optimized targeting was also available in conversion-focused Video campaigns, but those have recently been deprecated in favour of Demand Gen.)

Remember, you don't want to use Optimized targeting in a remarketing campaign because remarketing is supposed to show ads to people who already have a relationship with your business. Optimized targeting is going to find people who, for the most part, aren't on your remarketing list. If you want to use your remarketing list as a *signal* for Google to find new users who are similar to your existing ones, then you can:

- add your remarketing list to your campaign targeting, then turn Optimized targeting on
- create a Lookalike segment in a Demand Gen campaign, based on your remarketing list

One of the top things I look for when I audit a Google Ads account is whether or not Optimized targeting is turned on. To check, go to Audiences, keywords and content > Audiences and expand the section called "Audience segments." This is where you can see how each of the audience segments in your campaign or ad group are performing.

At the bottom of the Audience segments chart, you'll find a few summary rows in grey. The first is called Total: Segments, which shows you how your chosen audience segments are performing overall. Below that, you'll see Total: Expansion and optimized targeting, and if you see any data in this row at all, even if it's only a few impressions, that means Optimized targeting is turned on. Based on how it's meeting your goals, you can decide whether to leave Optimized targeting on or turn it off in your ad group settings.

How can you turn off Optimized targeting? It's surprisingly hidden in the Google Ads interface! Optimized targeting is set at the ad group level. If you want to turn it on or off, you won't find it under the Audiences tab. Instead, navigate to Campaigns > Ad groups, and hover your mouse over the Ad group name. Don't click on the name! Instead, click the little gear icon that pops up to pull up your Ad group settings. You will see an Optimized targeting checkbox, which you can select or unselect.

Some people swear by Optimized targeting, some people never use it, and honestly, so many Google Ads practitioners don't even know it exists. Regardless of how you feel about it, you should always check on your Optimized targeting!

When in doubt, I usually start by turning Optimized targeting off when launching image- and video-based campaigns. If my campaign targeting ends up being too niche and I'm having trouble serving, or I am serving ads but they're not converting well, then I may turn Optimized targeting on as a "boost." This can help me understand if the issue is my targeting, or something else. For example, if Optimized targeting starts driving good results, that means my targeting was off, which really means that I don't understand my target customer! If Optimized targeting doesn't drive good results, either, then perhaps my ad creative isn't enticing enough, my bid strategy is too restrictive, etc.

Audience expansion

Audience expansion is like Optimized targeting, but for reach-focused campaigns rather than conversion-focused campaigns. Just like Optimized targeting will show your ads to additional users, beyond your

WHAT ARE YOUR AUDIENCE TARGETING OPTIONS IN GOOGLE ADS?

audience selections, who are most likely to convert, Audience expansion will show your ads to additional users, beyond your audience selections, who are *relevant and can help increase your reach.*

This is one of those scenarios where, in my opinion, Google makes things way more complicated than they need to be. Most people probably don't even know that Audience expansion and Optimized targeting are two different things, and honestly, the distinction isn't terribly important. If you're in a Display, Demand Gen or Video campaign, you will either have access to Optimized targeting or Audience expansion. You will turn it on if you want to give up some control in exchange for increasing your reach, and you will turn it off if you want to maintain control over the audience segments who can see your ads.

Remember, Optimized targeting treats your audience *segments* as an Audience *signal* to find more users who are likely to convert. Audience expansion works a little differently, since it's used in campaigns without a conversion objective.

Here's a Jyll explanation rather than an official Google explanation: Audience expansion is like activating a Lookalike segment for your audience targeting.

Just as a Lookalike segment for your customer list will find users who behave similarly to your customers, Audience expansion finds users who behave similarly to those in your selected audience segments. For example, if you have an ad group that targets the In-market segment "Business Financial Services," Audience expansion may decide to also target the In-market segment "Business Loans" since those audiences are similar.

To check whether or not you have Audience expansion turned on, go to Audiences, keywords and content > Audiences and expand the section called Audience segments. This is where you can see how each of the audience segments in your campaign or ad group are performing. At the bottom of this chart, you'll find a few summary rows in grey. The first is called Total: Segments, which shows you how your chosen audience segments are performing overall. Below that, you'll see Total: Expansion and optimized targeting, and if you see any data in this row at all, that means Audience expansion is turned on (or Optimized targeting is turned on, if you're in a conversion-focused campaign). Based on how it's meeting your goals, you can decide whether to leave Audience expansion on or turn it off. Thankfully, turning Audience expansion off is much simpler than turning Optimized targeting off. You can adjust your Audience expansion settings in your ad group settings, or in your "Edit audience segments" window.

Full disclosure: I have never used Audience expansion in any of my campaigns, probably because I rarely run campaigns on a reach objective. If you're looking for a quick way to expand the reach of a Video campaign, either to hit campaign minimums or decrease CPMs, try checking the box for Audience expansion. Alternatively, you can pick additional audiences and add them to the campaign yourself; that's probably what I'd do rather than using Audience expansion.

Audience signal

We've already mentioned Audience signals in quite a few places throughout this book, so now it's time to give them their due. An Audience signal is an optional input you can add to your Performance Max campaign to "help Google AI optimize for your selected goals." Audience signals are added at the asset group level, and each asset group can only have 1 Audience signal.

WHAT ARE YOUR AUDIENCE TARGETING OPTIONS IN GOOGLE ADS?

From an ad targeting perspective, Performance Max is fully automated. You do not get to choose who sees your ads. When you add an Audience signal to an asset group in your Performance Max campaign, you are simply letting Google know who *you* think the right audience is for your ads. Your ads may or may not show to users who match your Audience signal. Google may say, "Thanks for the help, I'll check them out!" or something more like, "What an idiot. No thanks - ignore!"

(Google Ads won't actually talk to you, sadly, but I imagine this is what the artificial intelligence would say, if it could talk.)

This is why Audience signals and Optimized targeting are so interlinked in my brain, even though they are independent Google Ads concepts. Optimized targeting turns your audience *targeting* into an audience *signal*, and aims to find you users who are most likely to convert. An Audience signal lets you suggest audiences to Google's AI, but ultimately, it will show ads to whichever users it thinks are most likely to convert.

Sounds the same, right? Don't worry, the people who write the Google Ads Help Center get them confused, too. In an article about how to use Audience Builder, it says "All campaigns except Performance Max can use manual targeting. Performance Max campaigns use only optimized targeting."

To be super clear, despite what this article says, you cannot use Optimized targeting in a Performance Max asset group, only an Audience signal. But for all intents and purposes, *they do the same thing.*

If you'd like to know which audience segments your Performance Max campaigns are actually showing ads to, you can get a general idea from the Insights tab. Scroll down to the box labeled "Audience insight" to see how the people viewing your ads are different from the general population.

For example, you might see that 57% of your impressions come from people who are "In-Market for Advertising & Marketing Services," with an index of 2.8x. In plain English, this means that a little more than half of the time that your PMax ads showed, they showed to people who are currently in the market for advertising and marketing services.

What about the 2.8x index? The index thing is a mind melt, so I'm going to explain it first in a way that is simple, mostly accurate, but technically incorrect. Then, I will clarify by being 100% accurate, technically correct, but more confusing.

Okay, so the mostly true answer: a 2.8x index means that people who see your ads are 2.8x more likely than the general population to be in the market for advertising and marketing services.

Now, for the correction: the index is based on *impressions*, not on *people*. For example, if 10% of all Google Ads traffic comes from people who are in the market for advertising and marketing services, 2.8x times 10% means that 28% of your impressions are from people who are in the market for advertising and marketing services. Remember, impressions are not the same as people, since the same person can see your ads again and again and again.

My general rule of thumb is to only turn an insight into action if:
- The index is at least 3.0x
- Traffic from the general population for this audience segment is 10% or less

We'll explore this topic deeper in the "Audience insights" chapter, in the "How to use audiences" section of this book.

You can create an Audience signal within a Performance Max asset group, or from the Audience Builder in Audience Manager. Although an Audience signal is not the same thing as an Audience used for ad targeting, Google treats them interchangeably, and you'll find them "living together" on the Audiences tab in Audience Manager.

An Audience signal can have a few different components, each with their own unique requirements for Performance Max: Your data, Interests & detailed demographics, and Demographics:

- **Your data:** I highly recommend that you include Your data segments as part of your Audience signal. Note that while you can include the four kinds of Your data segments, you can't include a Custom combination in an Audience signal. Also remember that even if you don't explicitly add Your data segments to your Audience signal, they will still inform your campaign targeting and performance since Performance Max campaigns must use Smart Bidding, and Smart Bidding uses Your data segments as one of its many inputs. More on that when we get to "How audiences work with bidding."
- **Interests & detailed demographics:** This is where you can add any of Google's four audience types to your Audience signal, plus any Custom interests (the close cousin of Custom segments). Combined segments cannot be added to an Audience signal.
- **Demographics:** Right as this book went to print, Google announced that Demographic exclusions are coming for Performance Max as a beta. Until now, even though you could check or uncheck Demographic boxes in the Audience signals setup (for example, Age 18-24, Male, etc.),

this would previously have no impact on your campaign targeting. After all, an Audience signal is a signal, not targeting. That appears to be changing. However, as a beta, it's unknown if and when this could be rolled out to all accounts.

All of the Audience signals you create in a Google Ads account can be found under Tools > Shared Library > Audience Manager > Audiences. Even if you create them from within a Performance Max campaign, your Audience signals will be accessible at the account level. This means that your Audience signals can also be used as audience targeting in other campaign types that support the Audience Builder workflow, like Demand Gen. Beware that if you make a change to an existing Audience or Audience signal from one campaign, that change will be applied everywhere the Audience or Audience signal is being used.

Search Themes

Search themes are another optional Performance Max signal. While Audience signals "help Google AI optimize for your selected goals," Search themes are "an easy way to guide Performance Max to serve on placements that you may not be reaching yet."

Search themes are actually quite different from Audience signals, and not just because they are search-based. Search themes give you the opportunity to let Google know that there are certain kinds of searches you'd like to advertise on, even if those keywords aren't highlighted on your landing page or in your feed.

For example, let's say you just launched a new product. Maybe you're a skincare company, primarily offering products for adults, and you just launched a new line of skincare for teens. Google may not "recognize" searches for teen skincare as relevant for your business, at least not right away. To compensate, you could add Search themes like "skincare for teens" "safe acne treatments" "all natural face cream" etc. to *nudge* Google to start serving on those types of searches.

Another example: competitor targeting. Let's say you want your Performance Max to be eligible to show ads when someone searches for your competitors. If you want the campaign to *only* show ads when someone searches for your competitor, you could add brand restrictions in your campaign settings. But let's say you want those competitor searches to be included alongside whatever other searches you're serving ads on. You could add your competitors' names as Search themes, to nudge Google into showing ads on searches related to your competitors.

Remember, Search themes are optional, and Performance Max campaigns will ultimately choose whatever ad targeting is needed to meet the objective of your bid strategy. Because of this, it's not clear to me that Search themes will actually help you drive better results. Here's why.

If your Performance Max campaign is *already serving* on the searches you want, then you don't need Search themes. PMax has it covered. You can check this by looking at your Search terms Insights under Insights and reports > Insights.

If your Performance Max campaign *is not already serving* on the searches you want, then Search themes are a Band-Aid, not a solution. Search themes are just a signal, and Performance Max will always default to showing your ads to *whoever is most likely to convert*. If Google doesn't recognize certain searches as being relevant for your business, then advertising on those searches will probably be *less profitable* than advertising on searches that Google *does* recognize as being related to your business. For example, in the "launching a new product" scenario, your conversion rate for a new product will probably be a lot lower than your conversion rate for existing, tried-and-true products. In the "competitor targeting" scenario, your conversion rate on searches for your competitors will probably be a lot lower than your conversion rate on searches for *your* brand.

What can you do instead of Search themes, if Performance Max isn't serving ads on the searches you'd like? Run a Search campaign. That would be the obvious choice! If you do want to stick with PMax, I recommend starting a separate campaign, so that you can have a separate budget dedicated to this "untapped" area, and potentially different Smart Bidding targets to achieve that goal.

One thing that you should check is whether or not Google understands what your landing page or your website are all about. The Search component of Performance Max is powered by Dynamic Search Ads technology, and there's a quick little trick to figure out the types of searches that DSA will match you to, before launching a campaign. Open up Keyword Planner under Tools > Planning > Keyword Planner, then choose "Start with a website." Type in your landing page, or your whole website if you're using final URL expansion, and see what keywords come up. If these seem like the right kinds of keywords for your business, then congratulations! The Search part of PMax is likely to do what you want it to do. If these do not seem like the right kinds of keywords for your business, then:

- The Search part of PMax is unlikely to do what you want it to do

- Search themes won't hurt, so you should definitely add them to your PMax campaign
- Work with an SEO consultant to improve your website's content, structure, etc. so that Google will gain a better understanding of your business, and place your PMax ads accordingly

You can use up to 25 Search themes per asset group. Just like with keywords, you can include competitor names in your Search themes.

The best way to think about Search themes is as a replacement/upgrade for a searches-based Custom segment, since you can no longer include Custom segments in your Audience signals, only Custom interests. Video campaigns got Custom search terms as a replacement, and Performance Max campaigns got Search themes.

Remember, though, that Custom search terms in a Video campaign are a form of *targeting*: when used, you will show ads to people who have searched for those things. In contrast, Search themes in a Performance Max campaign are a *signal*: when used, you are letting AI know the types of users you're interested in, but ultimately, Google will show your ads to whomever is likely to help it meet your campaign objective, whether or not those users are searching for your Search themes.

Another key difference is that Custom search terms are purely audience targeting. By adding a Custom search term to your Video campaign, you are not choosing the kinds of YouTube searches you might show ads on (if your campaign subtype shows ads on YouTube search results). You are showing ads to *people who have searched for certain things, but are not searching right now - they're watching videos right now.*

Search themes, however, can influence the Search inventory and non-Search inventory for your Performance Max campaign. By adding Search themes, your Performance Max campaign could start showing ads to people searching for those terms, *when they're searching*, and it could start showing ads to people *who have searched for those terms* while they're watching videos, playing with apps, or otherwise minding their own business online.

Google says that "Search themes can do everything that Custom segments do in Performance Max, and more." With slight modifications to this statement, I agree. Jyll says that "Search themes can do everything that *searches-based* Custom segments *used to* do in Performance Max, and more."

Recapping what's changed for Performance Max signals:
- Custom segments that were based on searches were upgraded to Search themes
- Custom segments that were based on interests, websites and/or apps were upgraded to Custom interests, which you can include in an Audience signal

Keyword prioritization and Search themes
Keyword prioritization is how Google chooses which of your ads to show when a user searches for something that's relevant to your business.

It occurred to me while writing this chapter that Search themes are a funny little thing since they are both an audience *signal* and a content *signal*. To ensure we appreciate the full impact of using or not using optional Search themes in Performance Max, let's take a brief detour into keyword prioritization rules.

WHAT ARE YOUR AUDIENCE TARGETING OPTIONS IN GOOGLE ADS?

There are many different ways that Search campaigns and Performance Max campaigns can become eligible to show ads when a user searches for something on Google. These include:
- Keywords, added to a Search campaign in Broad, Phrase or Exact Match
- Search themes, added to a Performance Max campaign
- Dynamic ad targets, added to a Dynamic ad group in a Search campaign
- AI-matching, for Performance Max campaigns without Search themes

When a user searches for something, and your Google Ads account has multiple Search keywords, Search dynamic ad targets, Performance Max Search themes and/or Performance Max asset groups without Search themes that are eligible to show an ad, keyword prioritization kicks in to determine which one will "move forward" to the auction and represent your business. Remember, your Google Ads account can only enter each ad auction once, so you want to put your best foot forward every time.

Exact Match keywords that are *identical* to the user's search will always get first priority to enter the auction. Broad Match keywords, Phrase Match keywords and Performance Max Search themes that are *identical* to the user's search share second priority. When there is no identical match, "AI prioritization" takes over, which is a fancy way of saying Google tries to determine which of your campaigns has the most relevant match for the user's search. This will get third priority. Final prioritization rule: when multiple options have the same priority - for example, if you have a Broad Match keyword and a Performance

Max Search theme that are both *identical* to the user's search - then the one with the higher Ad Rank will move forward to the auction. Good old Ad Rank!

Why have we taken this detour in a book about audience targeting? Keyword prioritization affects how we think about the role of Search themes in three key ways.

First, when the user's search is identical to your keyword or Search theme, Exact Match keywords will beat Performance Max Search themes every time, but Phrase Match and Broad Match won't. This means that if you are also running Search campaigns in your account alongside Performance Max, the decision to add or not to add Search themes, and which 25 Search themes to prioritize, is intertwined with the decision about which match types to use. For example, if you want Search to always win over PMax, Exact Match keywords are the way to ensure Search's victory more frequently. However, if you want the ad with the highest Ad Rank to always win, Phrase or Broad Match keywords plus Search themes would be a better option, as they all share equal priority.

Second, if you don't add Search themes, then Search campaigns will beat out Performance Max every time that there's an identical match to the user's search. Search themes help PMax have a better chance at *winning* on search inventory. If you're trying to test Search vs Performance Max, keep this dynamic in mind and consider using Google's in-platform Experiments tool for a fair A/B test.

Third, there are billions of searches a day on Google. Most of the time, there will not be an identical match in your account for the user's search. While misspellings are still considered an identical match, plurals are not, and synonyms are definitely not. In practice, this means that the third priority "AI prioritization" will take over most of the time, and if your Performance Max campaign is determined to have a higher Ad Rank than a Search campaign, even if you have a Search keyword like "google ads course" and the user searches "google ads courses" and your Performance Max has no Search themes, Performance Max could "win" and move forward to the auction.

Say all this to say - the days of SKAGs (single keyword ad groups) and tight control are long gone, regardless of what keyword match type you're using in your Search campaigns, whether or not you're running Performance Max, and whether or not you use Search themes.

Lookalike segments

Lookalike segments are groups of users who share similar online behaviour to Your data segments. Before you get too excited, you can only create and use Lookalike segments in a Demand Gen campaign.

Given that Demand Gen campaigns are Google's answer to "let's make it really easy for Meta media buyers to spend money with Google," Lookalike segments in Google Ads will feel very familiar to you if you've ever set up and used a Lookalike audience in Meta Ads.

To create a Lookalike segment, you must have a new or existing Demand Gen campaign, and you must be in a Demand Gen ad group, in Audience Builder. Lookalike segments live within an Audience (capital A). If you want to *only* target ads to your Lookalike segment, then ensure it's the only audience segment you include in your Audience. If you want to target ads to your Lookalike segment and other audiences, you can add them all in the same Audience; your Demand Gen ad group will break out audience segment reporting for you. If you'd like to show different ad creative to your Lookalike segment vs the other audiences you're targeting then you'll need to put them in different Audiences, in different ad groups.

To create a new Lookalike segment, you'll need to give it a name and then tell Google three things: seed list, location, and reach profile.

1. Seed list(s)
The purpose of a Lookalike segment is to find new users who are similar to users your business already knows: a remarketing list. For example, your customers, your YouTube subscribers, your email newsletter members, etc. To create a Lookalike segment, you need to choose which Your data segment(s) to use as your "seed list(s)," aka which type of users you'd like the algorithm to go out and find more of.

You can choose one Your data segment as the seed for your Lookalike segment, or many. The maximum is 10 seed lists per Lookalike segment.

If your seed lists are quite large - say, at least 10,000 active matched users per list (you can check this in Audience Manager) - then I recommend using just one seed list per Lookalike. You can then create multiple Lookalikes with different seed lists, and test them out in different ad groups to see which perform best.

If your seed lists are quite small - perhaps a few hundred or few thousand active matched users each - then you may want to group multiple seed lists together in one Lookalike segment, to ensure there's enough data for Google to figure out what they have in common, and who it should show ads to based on that.

Lookalikes should be seeded with your *best* remarketing lists. For example, someone who is a customer or an app user is much more engaged with your business than someone who viewed one YouTube video. I probably wouldn't use such a casual audience, like YouTube video viewers, as a seed list for a Lookalike segment, even though it's likely to be one of your largest lists.

Your best seed lists for Lookalike segments are likely to be:
- **Customers**: Any and all Customer Match lists
- **Website**: Purchases, Form Fills, Highly Engaged Visitors. Don't use all website visitors as a seed for Lookalikes, it's too broad.
- **App**: All app users. If someone downloads and opens your app, they are more engaged than 99% of the people who will interact with your business.
- **YouTube**: Subscribers. Anything less than tapping Subscribe is too casual an action to hold enough value for a Lookalike. Don't worry, those viewers are very valuable for other audience targeting purposes!

The users on your Lookalike segment will refresh every 1-2 days and adjust based on any changes to your seed list. For example, if you're running a lot of YouTube ads and getting hundreds of new subscribers a day, that data will inform a Lookalike segment whose seed list is YouTube subscribers. The Lookalike will continue to analyze new and old subscribers as the seed list grows, and adjust who it wants to categorize as most similar.

A caution about list size: There must be at least 100 active matched users across your seed lists in order for the Lookalike segment to be eligible to build (and serve).

2. Location

Lookalike segments are country-specific. If your Demand Gen campaign is targeting Mexico, then your Lookalike country should be Mexico. If your Demand Gen campaign is targeting New York, Chicago and Los Angeles, then your Lookalike country should be the United States. If your Demand Gen campaign is targeting New York and Toronto, you could set your Lookalike countries as United States and Canada; however, you may want to launch country-specific Demand Gen campaigns instead. In this example, you could have Demand Gen (New York) with a Lookalike segment based in the United States, and Demand Gen (Toronto) with a Lookalike segment based in Canada.

3. Reach

Warning: what I'm about to explain is the most confusing part of Lookalike segments, and I'd even put it on the list of top 5 most confusing things in all of Google Ads.

We've made it this far together, so let's go for it.

When you create a Lookalike segment, it doesn't just say, "Okay, I'll go find more people in your chosen country who are similar to those on your seed list." No. What it actually says is, "Okay, I'll go find the 5% of Canadians who are most similar to those on your seed list" or "Okay, I'll go find the 2.5% of French, German, Spanish and Italian users who are most similar to those on your seed list." This is why the country or countries you input as part of the Lookalike segment creation are so important.

Your reach options are 2.5% (Narrow), 5% (Balanced - the default) and 10% (Broad). Call me old fashioned, but I'll usually pick the most narrow option, 2.5% - as you'll see, even that can end up being very, very broad.

WHAT ARE YOUR AUDIENCE TARGETING OPTIONS IN GOOGLE ADS?

Let's illustrate with an example of Canada (Population: 39 million) and the United States (Population: 333 million). Although active matched users on Google will be lower than the real-life population, population is a simple proxy for understanding how this all works.

If I create a Lookalike segment based on my customer list, targeting Canada, at 2.5% reach, that means that Google will find the 2.5% of Canadians who are most similar to my customers, based on their online behaviour. 2.5% of 39 million is just under 1 million people, so my Demand Gen campaign would be eligible to reach about a million people. A million! Unless I'm a very large business, it's unlikely that there are a million people in Canada, or even half a million people in Canada, who would be interested in what I'm selling. This is using the "Narrow" setting, mind you - not even Balanced (5%) or Broad (10%).

If I create a Lookalike segment based on my customer list, targeting the United States, at 2.5% reach (Narrow), that means that Google will find the 2.5% of Americans who are most similar to my customers, based on their online behaviour. 2.5% of 333 million is 8.3 million, so my Demand Gen campaign would be eligible to reach about 8 million people. Although my potential market size in the United States would be larger than my potential market size in Canada, if I'm a small business or a B2B business or a niche business, it's unlikely that even 1 million Americans would be interested in what I'm selling, nevermind 4 million or 6 million or 8 million.

Now, before we freak out and write off Lookalike segments as useless, remember that these segments are country-wide. Although my Canadian Lookalike segment may have a million people on it, perhaps my Demand Gen campaign is only targeting Toronto. (About 8% of Canadians live in Toronto.) If my seed list, my customer list, had users from across the country, we could reasonably expect that about 8% of the users on my Lookalike segment will be in Toronto, too. 8% of 1 million is 80,000. Even though the Lookalike segment is built based on a whole country, your ads will only serve to users in the locations you choose to target from your campaign. In this case, about 80,000 potential users.

Then, remember that Demand Gen campaigns only show ads on YouTube, Gmail, Discover, and Video partners (if you have them enabled). Are all 80,000 potential users going to be active on those Google platforms in a given day, week or month? No, they're not. If I had to pull a guess out of thin air, I'd say we might get a unique reach of 40,000 or so in Toronto, from this Demand Gen campaign, over the course of a month, with a four-figure budget.

I say all this to say: Lookalike segments are a useful tool. They are not some magical solution that is guaranteed to find you the perfect new customers, especially if you're targeting a larger country. Try them. Test them. They may drive great results for your Demand Gen campaign, or they may dramatically underperform more focused audience targeting options like a Custom segment based on searches. But there's only one way to find out!

Hot tip: It can take a couple of days for a new Lookalike segment to "ramp up" and start spending, so don't freak out (yet) if you set the campaign live and get zero impressions for a few days. If you're planning a new Demand Gen campaign, it's a good idea to build your campaign and create your Lookalike segment as soon as possible, even if you don't have your creative, budget, etc. sorted yet. Once your Lookalike segment is created, it will start analyzing and building, even if the campaign isn't live yet. Then, once you do have everything else ready to go a few days or weeks later, your Lookalike segment should be ready to serve when you enable your campaign.

What happened to Similar segments?
Before we move on from Lookalike segments, I'd be remiss if I didn't mention the elephant in the room: Similar segments. Similar segments, formerly known as Similar audiences, were deprecated in 2023.

Why bother dredging up an old audience targeting feature that doesn't exist anymore? Because it *doesn't exist anymore*. Lookalike segments are *not* the same thing as Similar segments. In this book, we've explored some audience targeting capabilities where features have been renamed, rebranded, reimagined, but essentially do the same thing. This is *not* one of those circumstances.

When they existed, Similar segments were *automatically-created* audience segments based on *each* of Your data segments. You could use Similar segments across most campaign types, including Search, Display, Demand Gen and Video. They were *not* country-specific. You did *not* choose a Narrow/Balanced/Broad reach profile. The only similarity that both Similar segments and Lookalike segments share is that they find new users who are similar to those on your remarketing lists.

If you're trying to achieve the effect of a Similar segment today, or a Lookalike segment outside of a Demand Gen campaign, you can try:
- Optimized targeting in Display (or Demand Gen). This will find users who are most similar to your *converters* rather than users who are most similar to your *remarketing lists*. At the end of the day, that's what you want anyway, right? New users who are most likely to become customers?
- Audience expansion in Video. This will find users who

are most similar to those you're currently targeting, if you want to expand your reach. The poorest substitute, in my opinion, but an option worth mentioning if your measure of success is something like reach, unique reach or frequency, and not conversions.
- New customer acquisition goal in Performance Max, Shopping or Search. This campaign-level setting will use your remarketing lists as a signal, and then find new users who are most likely to become customers. If you see that your Performance Max campaign is doing a lot of remarketing and you want to "kick it" into prospecting instead, test out New customer acquisition - but expect a drop in conversion rate, accordingly.

App campaigns (Exclusion only)

I warned you at the beginning of this book that we would not be discussing App campaigns much. Partly because I haven't personally worked with an App campaign since 2022, but mostly because you don't get to choose any audience targeting for an App install campaign. Google shows your ads to whoever it likes, for whatever reason it likes, without telling you a single detail about it.

What you can do, however, is add audience *exclusions* to an App campaign. For example, if you want to ensure you don't show ads to certain remarketing lists, or to users of other apps you own, you can achieve this by excluding Your data segments.

It's also worth mentioning that App campaigns for engagement will *only* target people who have your app installed. After all, you can't engage with an app you don't have on your phone! App campaigns are also smart enough to not show install ads to people who already have your app installed on their phone. After all, you can't install an app twice!

In summary, App campaigns are pretty smart, and are designed to drive performance at scale with minimum human input.

Now, I will return to not talking about App campaigns.

☐ Remember this! Types of automated targeting in Google Ads

Optimized targeting: turns your audience segments into an audience signal. Google will show your ads to whomever it thinks is most likely to convert

Audience expansion: expands your reach by targeting additional audience segments beyond those you've selected

Audience signals: optional Performance Max input to help guide the automation. Google will still show your ads to whomever it thinks is most likely to convert

Search themes: optional Performance Max input to help guide the automation towards inventory that Google may not recognize as being related to your final URL

Lookalike segments: groups of people that share similar characteristics to Your data segments, for Demand Gen campaigns only

App campaigns (Exclusion only): you can't choose any audience targeting for inclusion, but you can exclude Your data segments

Cheat Sheet: Automated targeting

	Search	Shopping	Display	Video	Demand Gen	PMax
Optimized targeting	X	X	✓	X	✓	X
Audience expansion	X	X	X	✓	X	X
Audience signals	X	X	X	X	X	✓
Search themes	X	X	X	X	X	✓
Lookalike segments	X	X	X	X	✓	X

How to use audiences in your Google Ads campaigns

CONGRATULATIONS! You now know everything about every single kind of audience targeting available to you in Google Ads.

Now, let's move into everything about *how to use* those audiences. We're going to discuss how audiences work with all the different campaign types in Google Ads, and explore some campaign-specific nuances - for example, Google owned properties in Demand Gen, or Remarketing Lists for Search Ads.

Display, Video and Demand Gen campaigns

Display, Video and Demand Gen are all visual campaign types that allow you to proactively put your ads in front of the kinds of people who are most likely to be interested in what you offer. Accordingly, these are the most common places you'll use audience targeting in Google Ads.

Display and Video campaigns

Display and Video campaigns in Google Ads allow you to show audience-targeted and/or content-targeted ads on millions of websites and apps across the internet. Collectively, those websites and apps are called the Google Display Network, and they reach more than 90% of Internet users around the world.

Display campaigns are primarily for image-based ads, while Video campaigns are primarily for video-based ads. However, you can also include video assets as an optional part of a Display campaign.

We typically call Video campaigns "YouTube campaigns," but this is a bit of a misnomer. Yes, you can run your Video campaign exclusively on YouTube (which is part of the Display Network), or you can opt into "Video partners," which will show your videos ads across the entire Display Network, not just on YouTube.

You can add audience and content targeting at the campaign level or the ad group level in Display and Video campaigns, for inclusion or exclusion.

Your content targeting options for Display and Video campaigns are Topics, Placements and Keywords.

- **Topics**: show ads to people *as they are engaging* with content about certain topics.
  - Topic examples: Outfit Inspiration, Business Formation, Condos & Townhomes
- **Placements**: show ads to people *as they are using* certain websites and apps, or *watching* certain videos/channels on YouTube.

- Placement examples: all Education apps, the Baby Phone app, searchenginejournal.com, Ms Rachel's YouTube channel, the "I Love a Rainbow with Ms Rachel and Elmo" video (that one's a favourite in my house right now).
- **Keywords**: show ads to people as they *search for or browse* content that's related to those terms.
  - Keyword examples: learn google ads, best neighbourhoods in toronto, winter boots for kids

Demand Gen campaigns

Demand Gen campaigns are an image- and video-based ad format that allow you to show audience-targeted ads on Google-owned properties: YouTube, Gmail and Discover.

Think of Demand Gen campaigns as analogous to running Meta Ads on Google platforms. In fact, Google originally created Discovery campaigns (the precursor to Demand Gen campaigns) as a competitive response to Facebook. My understanding, based on the sales narratives I was given while working at Google, is that Google was concerned about advertisers moving their ad dollars from Google to Facebook, or bypassing Google altogether to stick with Facebook's easier-to-use platform. To respond, Google launched Discovery campaigns to mimic the Facebook ad-buying process as closely as possible.

Although Discovery campaigns were all "upgraded" to Demand Gen campaigns, Demand Gen honours this legacy and still has some unique features that you won't find anywhere else in Google Ads (except for Performance Max, since PMax includes Demand Gen). These include:

- Carousel image ads
- Portrait images (4:5 aspect ratio)
- Lookalike segments
- Discover inventory
- Ad group-level budgets
- Ad group-level location and language settings

Google-owned properties

Google-owned properties, Google-owned surfaces, O&O (owned and operated) - this is all industry-speak for "websites and apps that Google owns."

Google Search, Gmail, Google Maps, YouTube are some examples of Google-owned properties that have more than a billion users each. Google owns dozens of different properties, and many of them support different kinds of ad placements, like Discover or Google Flights.

For Demand Gen campaigns, there are only 4 places your ads can show: 3 Google-owned properties, and optional Video partners, if you check that box (I never check that box).

The three Google-owned properties in Demand Gen are Discover, YouTube and Gmail. You're likely very familiar with Gmail and YouTube, but I wouldn't be surprised if "Discover" is a newer term for you.

Discover is a curated news feed of recommended content for Google signed-in users. The Discover feed can surface on Android phones from the home screen. If you're an Android user like me, you've definitely interacted with Discover, even if you didn't know that's what it's called. But Discover isn't Android-exclusive; it can also pop up in the Google Search app, which is available across devices, including iPhones.

Because Discover is predominantly mobile, the majority of YouTube watch time comes from mobile devices, and people check their email on mobile devices all day long, your Demand Gen campaigns are likely to serve ads more often on mobile devices than on desktop, tablet or TV screens. This is something to keep in mind as you're designing your ad creative; ensure it looks good on a small screen!

Demand Gen vs. Display campaigns
Demand Gen and Display campaigns have a lot in common. In a nutshell, the key difference is that Display campaigns are *more versatile* than Demand Gen, while Demand Gen campaigns produce *higher quality* results.

Let's start with the commonalities. Demand Gen and Display campaigns both:
- Support image- and video-based ads
- Proactively show your ads to users who are doing other things online
- Allow audience targeting
- Let you bid for a variety of objectives
- Can sync with your Merchant Center feed

However, Display lets you do some things that Demand Gen does not. In Display, you can use:
- Content targeting (Topics, Placements, Keywords)
- Combined segments
- Impression-based bid strategies
- Dynamic remarketing

So why do I prefer Demand Gen? Google-owned properties are the reason that Demand Gen campaigns are so powerful. Not just because of the exclusive inventory, but because they are *owned by Google*. Since Google owns Gmail, YouTube and Discover, and most of the users on those platforms are signed in to Google, the audience quality in Demand Gen tends to be very high since Google "recognizes" most of the users.

Compare that to Display campaigns, where your ads could show on YouTube or Gmail, but they're also going to show on millions of non-Google-owned websites and apps. Google will "recognize" many of those users, either due to cookies or logins, but Google will also *not* recognize many of those users. Google doesn't own those websites and apps, it just rents the ad space - Google is a third party in that relationship.

Nine times out of ten, I will recommend using Demand Gen over Display for your image- and video-based campaigns, to complement your Search campaigns by expanding your reach via audience targeting. The cost per click tends to be higher in Demand Gen than in Display, but still much lower than you'd get with Search. Given the corresponding audience quality on Google-owned properties, I generally find Demand Gen campaigns are worth it. The only reasons I'll recommend Display over Demand Gen these days are to access dynamic remarketing or Combined segments.

Audience compatibility with Display, Video and Demand Gen campaigns

Audience Type	Display	Demand Gen	Video
Your data segments		Yes	
Website visitors		Yes	
YouTube users		Yes	
App users		Yes	
Customer list		Yes	
Engaged audiences		Yes	
Custom combination		Yes	
Google's data		Yes (inclusion only in Demand Gen)	
Detailed demographics		Yes	
Affinity segments		Yes	
In-market segments		Yes	
Life Events		Yes	
Custom segments	Yes (inclusion only)		No*
Custom interests	No		Yes (incl. only)
Custom search terms	No		Yes (incl. only)
Combined segments	Yes (incl. only)		No*
Optimized targeting	Yes		No^
Audience expansion	No		Yes
Lookalike segments	No	Yes	No

* Video campaign audience features are currently changing. As I'm writing this, Custom segments and Optimized targeting are available in some Video campaigns. However, they are being phased out and will likely no longer be available within a few months of this book's release.

Audience attribution hierarchy

What happens when a user matches multiple audience targeting requirements? For example, they are in the market for SEO & SEM Services and they are also in the market for Web Design & Development? Or, they are on your customer list and your website remarketing list, and both of those segments are being targeted from the same campaign or ad group? Which audience segment gets "credit" for the impression, click and - hopefully - conversion?

In the "Automated targeting" section of this book, when we discussed Search themes, I introduced you to Google's keyword prioritization rules. Google has a similar prioritization playbook for audiences, which is called the Audience attribution hierarchy. Thankfully, the audience version is much simpler and more straightforward than the keyword version - however, it's also got a few gaps.

Here is how audience segments in Google Ads are prioritized for attribution, when a user belongs to multiple segments:

1. Customer Match
2. All other Your data segments and Lookalikes
3. Combined segments
4. Google's Affinity and In-Market segments
5. Google's Detailed demographics

What about then they match multiple segments? For example, two different In-Market segments? The one with the highest bid adjustment will get reporting and attribution credit, even if that bid adjustment was not used in the auction.

However, with Smart Bidding, are that many people really using bid adjustments these days? What happens then? ¯_(ツ)_/¯

And what about Custom segments or Life Events? ¯_(ツ)_/¯

Be careful what we wish for when we wish for Google to keep something simple!

Search & Shopping campaigns

Search and Shopping campaigns allow you to show ads when people search for things on Google. With Search ads, you can show text-based ads. With Shopping ads, you can show product-based ads.

Search and Shopping ads are shown using content targeting. In a Search campaign, you either select keywords or dynamic ad targets to tell Google the kinds of user queries you'd like to advertise on. In a Shopping campaign, you provide a feed of product information from Google Merchant Center, and then Google matches your ads with user queries based on the content of your feed.

As with Display and Video campaigns, you can use both content targeting and audience targeting together in Search and Shopping campaigns. A user needs to actually search for something in order for you to show an ad, so the content targeting is required via keywords, dynamic ad targets or feeds, but audiences are an optional and interesting add-on to these campaign types.

You can add audiences at the campaign level or the ad group level in Search and Shopping campaigns. Note that you cannot exclude audiences from Shopping campaigns.

Audience compatibility with Search and Shopping campaigns

Audience type	Search	Shopping
Your data segments	Yes	Yes
Website visitors	Yes	Yes
YouTube users	Yes	Yes
App users	Yes	Yes
Engaged audiences	Yes	Yes
Customer list	Yes	Yes
Custom combination	Yes	Yes
Google's data	Yes	Yes
Detailed demographics	Yes	Yes
Affinity segments	Yes	Yes
In-market segments	Yes	Yes
Life Events	No	No
Custom segments	No	No
Combined segments	Yes (inclusion only)	No
Automated targeting	No	No

Targeting vs. Observation

If you choose to add audiences to your Search or Shopping campaign, you can do so using Targeting or Observation.

Targeting *narrows your reach*. It means that you only want to show ads to users if they match both your content targeting AND your selected audience targeting. For example, if you add the Affinity segment "Business Professionals" on Targeting to a Search campaign, your ads can only serve if the user's search matches your content targeting AND they belong to the Business Professionals audience. If a user who is *not* a Business Professional (according to Google's understanding of them) searches for your exact keywords, they will not be eligible to see your ad.

Observation *collects data* and has no impact on reach. It means that you want to show your ads as usual, according to your content targeting selections, but if the user *also* belongs to one of the audiences you selected, keep track of that data. For example, if you add the Affinity segment "Business Professionals" on Observation to a Search campaign, your ads can serve to all users whose searches match your content targeting. If they are a Business Professional, they will be eligible to see your ad, and if they do, Google will keep track of their performance under a separate row in your Audience segment reporting. If they are not a Business Professional, they will be eligible to see your ad, and if they do, Google will group them under "Total: Other" in your Audience segment reporting, since they do not belong to your chosen audience segments.

Note that you can also select Targeting or Observation mode in Display campaigns. The use case here is a bit different; if you're using a manual bid strategy and you add audiences on Observation, you can then add bid adjustments on those audiences. You can also add Topics and Placements on Observation in a Display campaign, not just audiences. As someone who rarely, if ever, uses manual bidding, I'll freely admit that I've never used the Observation functionality in a Display campaign.

There's no reason *not* to add audiences on Observation to your Search and Shopping campaigns, though, since it doesn't affect performance yet allows you to collect additional user data. For this reason,

I always recommend adding a dozen or so audiences on Observation when you first launch a Search or Shopping campaign.

Pick audiences that you think may work well, or may *not* work well, and you'll start to see how they perform alongside your keywords / ad targets / feed. If a particular audience segment performs very well, you can consider launching a Display, Demand Gen or Video campaign targeting this segment. If a particular audience segment performs very poorly, you can consider excluding this segment from your Search campaign or ad group. (Unfortunately, you can't exclude audiences from Shopping campaigns.)

☑ **Remember this! Targeting mode vs. Observation mode**
Targeting means showing ads *only* if the user belongs to a selected audience segment.
Observation means showing ads as usual, and if the user belongs to one of the selected audience segments, include their metrics for reporting purposes.

Remarketing Lists for Search Ads (RLSA)

Remarketing Lists for Search Ads, also called RLSA, was all the rage when audience targeting capabilities were first added to Search and Shopping campaigns. Although you can apply most audience segments to Search campaigns, for Targeting or Observation, for inclusion or exclusion, there's something especially powerful and unique about combining Your data segments with search query targeting.

Here's how it works:
1. Create your Search (or Shopping) campaign

2. Choose your keywords, dynamic ad targets, feed, etc. as usual
3. Add remarketing audiences to your campaign or ad group on Targeting mode

Now, your ads will only show if the user's search matches one of your keywords *and* the user matches one of your audience selections. You can do this with any Your data segment: website, YouTube, app, Engaged audience, Customer Match, Custom combination.

One great use case for RLSA is to broaden your reach. For example, take all of your Search keywords and put them in Broad Match, but apply your remarketing audiences on Targeting. What this means is that you'll become eligible to serve on many more searches, but only if the user is already familiar with your brand, because they're on one of the remarketing lists.

Another way to use RLSA is to test previously unprofitable keywords that you think should be profitable. Would these keywords be profitable if you only serve ads to users who are familiar with your brand? For example, let's say you're a SaaS business that offers a free lead magnet. Paying money to advertise to someone looking for a free solution will likely be unprofitable, but what if that searcher has visited your website in the last 30 days? Then would you want to advertise? Similarly, let's say that you've tried competitor conquesting before and it was too expensive to sustain. Would those higher CPCs be worth it if you only advertised when your current or previous customers are searching for your competitors? What if you customized the ad text to offer a special incentive to stay with you?

This is generally how to think about Search and Shopping remarketing. Don't just use it to narrow yourself down into a hole. Instead, use it as a more conservative way to expand your reach.

Speaking of narrow, a third way to use RLSA is to narrow by exclusion. You can add Your data segments as exclusions in a Search campaign to avoid advertising to your existing customers, or to people who've recently visited your website. This can be an effective way to save money. For example, if a current customer is searching for "[your business name] login" then you probably don't need to spend money on an ad, your organic search results can be trusted to pick that up.

Be careful, though. Don't over-exclude Your data segments. If your current customers are searching for "[your business name] vs [competitor business name]" or "[your business name] alternatives," you definitely want to show an ad to try to retain them!

Performance Max campaigns

Audience targeting is showing ads to people based on who they are. By showing ads to certain types of people, you can feel confident that your Google Ads budget is going towards the most qualified users for your business.

Search, Shopping, Display, Demand Gen and Video campaigns all support audience targeting. You can pick the exact audiences you want to target, and the exact audiences you want to exclude, and your Google Ads campaigns will "obey" these choices and serve your ads accordingly.

Performance Max (and App campaigns) work differently. In Performance Max, the optional audiences you select work as a *signal* rather than as *targeting*. You are letting Google Ads know the types of users you'd like to reach, but ultimately, the AI driving the campaign could decide to listen to you, ignore you, whatever it wants to do to achieve your campaign objective.

In Performance Max, your campaign objective is determined by your bid strategy - and since it's Performance Max, you must pick an AI-powered Smart Bidding strategy. That means Maximize Conversions, Maximize Conversion Value, Target CPA or Target ROAS.

So what types of signals can you give PMax? You have the option to add an Audience signal and/or Search themes. You can select these signals (or choose not to) for each Asset group in your Performance Max campaign. Each Asset group can have up to 1 Audience signal and up to 25 Search themes. We explored Audience signals and Search themes in detail in the "Automated Targeting" section of this book, so if you've jumped ahead to this chapter, you may want to head back up there next.

☑ **Remember this! Audience targeting vs. Audience signal**
Audience targeting lets you show ads to certain types of people.
Audience signals let you tell Google what kind of people you'd like to show ads to, but ultimately, your ads will serve to whomever Google determines is most likely to convert.

☑ **Remember this! Search keywords vs. Search themes**
Search keywords let you tell Google the types of searches you'd like to show ads on.
Search themes let you tell Google up to 25 types of searches you'd like to show ads on, but ultimately, your ads will show up on whichever searches Google determines are most likely to lead to conversions.

App campaigns

App campaigns have been around much longer than Performance Max, and have given us a glimpse into the fully automated future that Google Ads has planned for all of us.

Like PMax, you must use a Smart Bidding strategy in App campaigns. Like PMax, targeting is fully automated for App campaigns. Like PMax, you can serve ads across all kinds of different inventory, covering both Google-owned and non-Google-owned properties, in a single campaign.

In an App campaign, your ads are eligible to serve on Google Search, Search partners, Google Play, YouTube, Gmail, Discover and the Google Display Network.

There are two main types of App campaigns. App install campaigns aim to reach new users and get them to download your app, while App engagement campaigns aim to reach users who already have your app downloaded, and get them to take some kind of in app action.

Performance Max works differently from Search, Shopping, Display, Demand Gen and Video campaigns because it only supports *signals* rather than true *targeting*.

In an App install campaign, targeting is fully automated - just like PMax. Audience signals are available for App install campaigns, too.

In an App engagement campaign, since these campaigns only target existing app users, that audience targeting is already "in place," so to speak. An app engagement campaign will only target users who have your app installed. You will have the option to target certain subsets of app users through your audience targeting, though. Some examples include:

- All app users

- Users who haven't opened the app recently
- Users who have opened the app recently
- Users who've taken specific actions within the app, like making a purchase

This is not an exhaustive list of all audience targeting options for App engagement campaigns, but you get the idea.

App campaigns are a large and profitable business for Google (source: the data I saw when I worked at Google), and on the whole, work effectively at driving advertiser's objectives. Performance Max has not been as warmly received as App campaigns were, even though the two campaign types are remarkably similar. Perhaps the user dynamics of an ecommerce purchase or a form completion are very different from the user dynamics of downloading an app or using an app. Perhaps the types of businesses who focus on apps have different mindsets, goals or objectives than your typical ecommerce or lead generation business.

In any case, the fact that we're seeing all kinds of increased transparency and control features being announced more than 2 years after PMax launched - like asset-level reporting and campaign-level negative keywords - is noteworthy, since we have not seen anything similar for App campaigns. These features weren't needed to drive App campaign adoption, whereas it appears they are absolutely needed to drive increased Performance Max campaign adoption.

Watch this space to see if Google brings PMax-type features, like brand exclusions, to App campaigns. The more likely outcome, in my opinion, is that App campaigns will be "upgraded" to Performance Max at some point, just like Smart Shopping and Smart campaigns and Smart Display campaigns.

Not so Smart after all, eh?

☑ Remember this! Google Ads campaign types

Search campaigns are a text-based ad format that allow you to show ads on user searches.

Shopping campaigns are a product-based ad format that allow you to show ads when people are searching for your products.

Display campaigns are an image- and video-based ad format that allow you to show audience-targeted and/or content-targeted ads on the Google Display Network.

Demand Gen campaigns are an image- and video-based ad format that allow you to show audience-targeted ads on YouTube, Gmail and Discover.

Video campaigns are a video-based ad format that allow you to show audience-targeted and/or content-targeted ads on YouTube and the Google Display Network.

Performance Max campaigns allow you to show Search, Shopping, Display, Demand Gen, Video and Local ads out of a single conversion-focused campaign. Targeting is fully automated.

App campaigns allow you to show text-, image- and video-based ads out of a single campaign focused on app installs or app engagement. Targeting is fully automated.

Audience insights

Audience insights is one of the most underrated features in Google Ads. It's one of my favourite "tricks" to pull out of my back pocket when I'm coaching an intermediate or advanced Google Ads practitioner.

Here's what you may not know: Audience Manager is not just the place where your audience segments live. It's also the place to get free insights about Your data segments.

In Google Ads, go to Tools > Shared Library > Audience Manager > Your data insights. Under "Segment to get insights on," you can click the pencil to choose which of Your data segments you'd like to analyze. As long as there are enough users on your segment, Google will tell you what it knows about them.

First, you can decide what to use as the benchmark for understanding what makes your audience unique. For example, when I look at my converters list, I can compare it to a benchmark of the United States, or a benchmark of the Google Display Network, which is a global audience. I'll usually pick a country rather than the global Display Network.

Next, you can see how the users on your list compare to that benchmark demographically. For example, my converters skew more female than the US population.

Finally, you can scroll down and see the really powerful stuff. Google will show you which In-Market segments and Affinity segments the users on Your data segment belong to, and how that compares to the benchmark. For example, the top In-Market segment for my converters list is In-Market for SEO & SEM Services. Okay, not a huge shock - but that's actually useful information. It confirms that my ads have reached the right audience.

Next to that, I see an Index of 7.3x, and if I hover my mouse on that number, Google tells me that 86% of my converters belong to this In-Market segment, vs. 12% of the United States. In plain English, an index of 7.3x means that my converters are 7.3x more likely than the benchmark (Americans) to belong to the In-Market segment for SEO & SEM Services. Is that meaningful? I like to see an index of at least 3x before I'll consider acting upon these insights, so in my opinion, this one is meaningful.

The percentage of the benchmark population is also important to keep in mind, as it puts the Index in context. For example, right now, my converter list shows a 3x index for Cat Lovers and for Dog Lovers. Great, let's run ads to Cat Lovers and Dog Lovers, right? Well, the benchmark tells me that 17% of Americans are Cat Lovers and 20% are Dog Lovers. Even though my converters are 3x more likely than the average American to be Cat and/or Dog Lovers, I wouldn't use that to target ads because 1 in every 5 Americans belongs to these segments! It's too broad, and likely a coincidence due to the sheer volume of pet lovers, rather than something unique about my converters. If I'm working with a small- to medium-sized business, I like to see a benchmark population percentage at around 10% or lower before I'll consider using one of these audiences for prospecting. In-Market segments tend to be more narrow than Affinities.

Some of your insights may look really wonky. For example, a few years ago, I was showing this to a client and we saw that In-Market: Trips to Moscow was a top segment. This company sold clothing. I don't think that a lot of the people who were converting on that website were in the market for trips to Russia. No, I think that the audience was reading news about the war that had recently broken out between Russia and Ukraine. Google's AI got confused, it didn't know enough about current events yet to know that this was noise, not a real signal. It's a good reminder that even artificial intelligence as advanced as Google's is just that: artificial. It lacks nuance and cultural understanding. It doesn't mean it's all bad! But do trust your gut and if something seems off, ignore it and move on.

The best remarketing list to look at under Audience insights will be your customer list. This is one of the many reasons I recommend uploading your customer list to Google Ads, even if you're not yet eligible to use Customer Match for ad targeting purposes. As long as your list is large enough, which usually means at least 1300 or so records, you can glean valuable insights from your customer list and incorporate that into your audience strategy, targeting strategy and overall marketing strategy.

A very similar audience insights functionality exists with Performance Max campaigns, and I also find this to be immensely helpful. In your PMax campaign, select from the left-hand menu Insights and reports > Insights, and then scroll down to the box labeled "Audience insight." Just like the Your data segments insights we saw above, this will tell you how the people viewing your PMax ads are different from the general population.

For example, you might see that 57% of your impressions come from people who are In-Market: Advertising & Marketing Services, with an index of 2.8x. In plain English, this means that a little more than half of the time that your PMax ads showed, they showed to people who are currently in the market for advertising and marketing services. What about the 2.8x index? Well, 57% / 2.8 = 20%, so that means that about 20% of Google Ads traffic, in general, comes from people who are in the market for advertising and marketing services. Since 57% of your impressions are from people who are in the market for advertising and marketing services, and 20% of general Google Ads impressions are from people who are in the market for these services, your impressions from this audience segment are 2.0x higher than would be expected from the general population.

My general rule of thumb is to only turn an insight into action if:
- The index is at least 3.0x
- Traffic from the general population for this audience segment is 10% or less

How audiences work with...

WHETHER YOU'VE BEEN working in Google Ads for 6 minutes, 6 months or 6 years, you've probably noticed that nothing operates in a vacuum. There are so many factors that contribute to campaign performance. Making a change to your keywords can completely change how your ad text performs, making a change to your conversion tracking can completely change how your bid strategy performs, and making a change to your ad group structure can completely change how your keywords perform.

The last step before I show you how to build an effective audience targeting strategy is to understand how audiences interact with your bidding, creative and conversion tracking, because it's not always intuitive.

Then, we'll bring everything together so you can build an audience targeting strategy that will be uniquely powerful for your business.

How audiences work with bidding

Smart Bidding in Google Ads means AI-powered, conversion-driven, and millions of signals. When you choose a Smart Bidding strategy for your campaign, rather than a manual bid strategy, you are communicating your goal to Google, and allowing the platform to dynamically set your bids for each and every auction to get you your desired results.

For example, choosing a Maximize Conversions bid strategy tells Google, "Here's my money. Do whatever you need to do with my money to get me as many conversions as possible within my budget."

I'm a huge proponent of Smart Bidding. There are many reasons to use Smart Bidding, which is the topic for a whole other book. As it relates to the topic of *this* book, Smart Bidding and audience targeting work beautifully together, since the AI will use your audience segments as a signal to help it achieve your goal.

Yes, your audience segments are not just a signal when you're using Optimized targeting or an Audience signal; they're also a signal for every single campaign in your account that's using Smart Bidding.

Let's say you've uploaded a list of customer email addresses into your Google Ads account. Whether or not you're actively leveraging Customer Match, the mere fact that this list exists means that all of your Smart Bidding strategies will use your customer data as an input to determine your bids. Your data makes the algorithm *smarter*.

Other Smart Bidding signals include device, time, day, location, language, browser, operating system, and many more. Plus, Smart Bidding uses data from across your account to set bids, not just the data that lives within a single campaign.

Smart Bidding + Audiences = Better together.

☐ Remember this! Smart Bidding strategies

Maximize conversions will aim to get you as many conversions as possible within your budget. The primary goal is spending the budget, and then getting conversions.

Target CPA will aim to get you conversions at your desired efficiency, your target cost per conversion. The primary goal is efficiency. If the campaign can't consistently hit your target CPA, it will stop spending. If it can, it will ask you for as much budget as it needs to maximize the opportunity.

Maximize conversion value will aim to get you as much revenue as possible within your budget. The primary goal is spending the budget, and then getting conversions - however, unlike Maximize conversions, it predicts the value of each conversion, and bids more for conversions it anticipates will be more valuable.

Target ROAS will aim to get you conversions at your desired efficiency, your target return on ad spend. The primary goal is efficiency. If the campaign can't consistently hit your target ROAS, it will stop spending. If it can, it will ask you for as much budget as it needs to maximize the opportunity.

How audiences work with creative

We've discussed the fact that audience targeting in Google Ads is moving farther away from *targeting* and more towards *signals*.

Well, perhaps at this point that's still my opinion, or my observation, rather than absolute fact, but we can at least say it's an undeniable trend.

What this means for you is that your ad creative now has an outsized impact on your campaign performance. In a signal-driven world, it's imperative to craft ads that appeal to your target audience, and don't appeal to your *not* target audience.

I call this "creative-led targeting," because you can use your text, image and/or video assets to "steer" the automation much more effectively than Optimized targeting or an Audience signal or Search themes on their own.

For example, let's say that you sell organic dog food, and you have two image ad creatives: an adorable golden retriever "smiling" straight at the camera, and the same golden retriever eating out of their dog bowl. What will happen if you use both images in a Performance Max asset group?

Tons of people who don't have a dog, and have no interest in your organic dog food, would engage with the first ad, because dogs are cute! Who doesn't like dogs? (I don't like dogs, actually, but I still think a picture of a dog is cute.)

If we can purely rely on audience targeting to only reach dog owners, then no problem - use the picture of a cute dog. But in a world where the ad platform is using automated targeting, analyzing user behaviour to determine who to show our ads to next, a widely appealing cute dog is a big problem. We're going to blow our budget showing off a cute dog, not attracting dog owners who want to try a new organic dog food. Will your PMax campaign eventually figure this out? Hopefully, but not before you've wasted a lot of money figuring it out.

Contrast this with the second image, a dog eating the food. This would not be as widely appealing, and would be more likely to grab the attention of current or aspiring dog owners, not mere dog lovers. It would appeal to your target audience, but just as importantly (if not more importantly), it would *not* appeal as much to your *not* target audience of people who think dogs are cute, but don't have a dog and aren't in the market for a new kind of dog food. Your PMax campaign will "find" those organic-loving dog owners faster, and you'll waste less money.

Why is creative-led targeting so important? It all comes down to human behaviour. People who are interested in your ads will engage with them, and Google Ads will try to find more people like them. People who are not interested in your ads will not engage with them, and Google Ads will no longer try to find people like them.

Creative-led targeting is how you teach the algorithm what it needs to know. Even though it has nothing to do with an Audience signal, it's the ultimate signal about what kind of audiences will drive great results for you.

How audiences work with conversion tracking

A conversion is the thing you want someone to do after interacting with your ad. For most ecommerce businesses, a conversion is a purchase. For most lead generation businesses, a conversion is a phone call, a lead form submission or an appointment booking.

Conversion tracking is how your business lets Google Ads know that a conversion has occurred, that something good happened, that the campaign is performing well.

Since so many Google Ads features rely on conversion tracking (Smart Bidding, Optimized targeting, campaign reporting, and on and on), it's important to have accurate conversion tracking for your account. Google Ads conversion tracking can be implemented in many different ways, including Google Analytics, the Google tag, Google Business Profile integration, call tracking software, third-party tool integrations, etc.

I've noticed over the years that the concepts of audience segments and conversion actions can often be confused. Let's ensure we've got that cleared up now, so we can explore how they interact with each other.

An audience segment, or audience list, is *a group of people* who match certain behaviours. They may be the people who've visited your website before, the people who are about to retire, the people who have recently searched for your competitors, or the people who've purchased from you within the last 30 days.

A conversion action is *a specific event* that is meaningful to your business, like a purchase or a phone call or a lead.

You can create an audience segment of *people who have completed that event*. The event might be "Purchase" (conversion action) and the group might be "All Purchasers (30 days)" (audience segment).

When you are tracking conversions, you're not paying attention to or keeping track of *who* took action, you're keeping track of the action itself: how often it happened, which campaigns caused it to happen, how much value it brings, and on and on. The focus is on the *action*.

When you are building an audience segment, you're not focused on the specific event or behaviour. You're keeping track of *who did that* so you can show ads to them at a later date.

There is a relatively new feature in Google Ads called Conversion-based customer lists that beautifully combines conversion tracking with audience segments.

Conversion-based customer lists

When we explored Customer Match, remarketing to your customer list on Google's platforms, we briefly mentioned something called Conversion-based customer lists. This Google Ads feature sits perfectly at the intersection of audience targeting and conversion tracking. I think this calls for another Venn diagram.

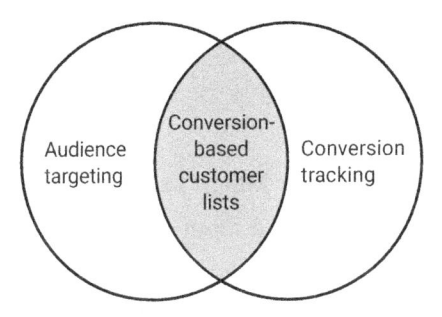

Conversion-based customer lists are a type of Customer Match audience segment that is built based on people who have converted, for each of your conversion goals.

In order to use Conversion-based customer lists, you must:
- have Enhanced conversions set up via the Google tag
- turn Conversion-based customer lists on in your Google Ads account settings, under Admin > Account Settings > Customer Match

In a previous example, I mentioned that you could have a conversion action for "Purchase" and an audience segment of "All Purchasers (30 days)." By activating Conversion based customer lists, you would not need to manually create the "All Purchasers (30 days)" audience in Google Analytics or Google Tag Manager. Google Ads would automatically create it for you using the data collected from your "Purchase" conversion action. If you have other conversion actions in the account, perhaps "Add to Cart" and "Email Newsletter Sign-up," then audience segments would be automatically created based on users who complete these conversion actions, too.

As with any Your data segment, once your Conversion-based

customer lists are large enough, you can use them for remarketing, as seed lists for Lookalike segments, or simply to analyze in your Audience insights.

Remember, any Customer Match list that exists in your account is automatically used as a data input for the machine learning that powers Smart Bidding and Optimized targeting. Even if you never add those Customer Match lists to a campaign or ad group, for Targeting or for Observation, the users on them will be examined and their behaviour will inform who Google chooses to show your ads to next, and how much it's willing to bid for them.

How to build an effective audience strategy

WE HAVE ARRIVED! We've learned about the difference between audience targeting and content targeting, every single type of audience segment you can use in Google Ads, how each audience type works with every campaign type, and how audiences interact with other key Google Ads features.

Now, let's bring it all together to build an effective audience targeting strategy for your business.

When you're working on a targeting strategy, regardless of whether you intend to use content targeting or audience targeting, you want to frame the opportunity in two ways:

1. How can I sell [offer] with Google Ads?
2. How can I reach [people] with Google Ads?

Let's compare and contrast these approaches with an easy, medium and difficult example, all taken from real Google Ads coaching clients I've worked with:

Easy example
How can I sell *dog food* with Google Ads?
How can I reach *dog owners* with Google Ads?

This example is simple because there is a clearly defined target audience (dog owners) for your product (dog food), and there are a plethora of ways you can reach this audience using both content and audience targeting.

Content targeting ideas:
- Search keywords around dog food, preferably longer tail keywords around the unique properties of this dog food (organic dog food, dog food delivery, etc.)
- Topics: Pet Food & Pet Care Supplies, Animal Products & Services
- Placements: topdogtips.com, caninejournal.com, pawsomerecipes.com, etc.

Audience targeting ideas:
- Life Event: Recently Added Dog to Household
- Life Event: Adding Dog to Household Soon
- In-Market: Pet Supplies
- Lookalike segment with seed list: Customer list

Medium example
How can I sell *Google Ads courses* with Google Ads?
How can I reach *Google Ads practitioners* with Google Ads?

   This example is medium difficulty because there are multiple potential target audiences for this product (Google Ads courses), so we'll start with just one of those audiences (Google Ads practitioners) for this strategy, and potentially build other strategies around other types of people. It's also medium difficulty because there is no pre-set Google audience for "Google Ads practitioners" as there is for "dog owners."

Content targeting ideas:
- Search keywords around google ads course, google ads training, learn google ads, etc., ensuring we stay away from / add negatives for things like free, certification, and other qualifiers that aren't relevant
- Topics: Search Engine Optimization & Marketing, Advertising & Marketing
- Placements: Barry Schwartz Search Engine Roundtable YouTube channel, Search Engine Land YouTube channel, Aaron Young YouTube channel

Audience targeting ideas:
- Custom segment (or Custom search terms) with the same search keywords as inputs
- Custom segment (or Custom interest) with app inputs like Google Ads, Google Analytics, Looker Studio, Meta Ads, etc.
- Non-linear option: Combined segment for In-Market for SEO & SEM Services AND In Market for Education AND

Life Event: Recently Started a New Job

Difficult example
How can I sell *engineering consulting services* with Google Ads?
How can I reach *mid-sized businesses looking to outsource their product design* with Google Ads?

This example is quite difficult because there are many kinds of target customers for these services, with no pre-set Google audience or content targeting options to reach them. We'll have to get creative and cast a wide net, knowing that our ideal customers will be swimming amongst plenty of non-ideal customers. This means our conversion tracking and Smart Bidding and ad creative will be doing a lot of heavy lifting alongside our targeting strategy.

Content targeting ideas:
- Search keywords around product design firm, engineering product design, outsourced product design - even better if we're naming the specific product we're trying to design, such as office chair design firm or outsourced textile design
- Topics: Industrial & Product Design, CAD & CAM, Engineering & Technology
- Placements: *websites for industry associations and conferences in the target industries of my ideal customers*

Audience targeting ideas:
- Custom segment (or Custom search terms) with the same search keywords as inputs
- Custom segment (or Custom interest) with the same

website placements as inputs

Audience exclusion as a strategy

Something to think about when you're building out your targeting strategy is audience and content exclusions, not just inclusions.

With keywords, you can add negative keywords to a Search, Shopping or Performance Max campaign to tell Google which searches you don't want to advertise on. Similarly, with audiences, you can add audience exclusions. Sometimes, crafting an exclusion strategy focused on who you *don't* want to reach can be an easier starting point than crafting an inclusion strategy focused on who you *do* want to reach.

A simple example: some people like to exclude an audience of recent purchasers from their remarketing campaigns, to avoid showing ads to people who've purchased their products within the last 30 days.

A more complex example: if you're looking to reach people who are not parents of children, you could target the "Not Parents" demographic. However, this will leave out the large "Unknown" segment. And it leaves a large question mark for someone who is a grandparent, or someone who is a parent, but their "child" is now an adult. Would Google classify them as a Parent or Not a Parent?

Instead, you can exclude the Detailed Demographics for Parents of Babies, Parents of Toddlers, etc. to ensure you're only keeping out people who are parents of children, but still including people who are parents of adults, grandparents, etc.

Non-Linear Targeting

To build an effective audience targeting strategy, you need to reach the kinds of people who are most likely to be interested in your offer.

Some kinds of people perfectly match a Google audience. For example, what if you sell mattresses, and you want to reach people who want to buy a mattress?

That's easy. Target the In-Market segment for mattresses.

I call this "Linear Targeting" because you are targeting exactly who you're looking for. It's as if you're an archer, and you shoot your arrow in a straight line directly into the bullseye. Target acquired.

But what if the kinds of people you want to reach don't perfectly match a Google audience? Or what if due to the niche-ness of your target customer, or personalized advertising policies, you don't have a straight-line path to reach your ideal audience?

Enter "Non-Linear Targeting," a term I coined to describe a strategy that takes an alternate route to reach your final destination. Think of this as being forced onto the scenic route while the main highway is under construction. It's not the ideal path, it will take longer than you anticipated, but it *will get you to your* final destination.

Let's look at our mattresses example. How might you build an audience strategy for a mattress company, using Linear and Non-Linear Targeting?

Linear Targeting
In-Market for Mattresses

Non-Linear Targeting
Life Event: Moving
Life Event: Marriage
In-Market: Home Furnishings > Bedroom

What if you sell something that has a not-quite-perfect-fit Google audience like... baby toys for newborns?

Linear Targeting
In-Market: Toys

Non-Linear Targeting
In-Market: Child Car Seats
In-Market: Strollers & Baby Carriages
In-Market: Home Furnishings > Nursery
Detailed demographics: Parents of Infants (0-1 years)

What if you sell something that does not fit any Google audience like... professional development courses for dental hygienists? (real client example, by the way)

Linear Targeting
???

Non-Linear Targeting
Custom segment (Custom search terms) with searches inputs such as periodontal charting, dental radiography training, and other job-specific terms.
Custom segment (Custom interest) with websites inputs such as American Dental Hygienists Association, etc.

What if you operate in a sensitive interest category, so you can't use custom segments? For example, let's say you're a plastic surgeon.

Linear Targeting
???

Non-Linear Targeting
Affinity: Beauty Mavens
In-Market: Anti-aging skincare
Life Event: Getting Married Soon

Now remember, even in a sensitive interest category, we can still leverage Optimized targeting (if we want to) and we can (and should) leverage Smart Bidding.

The most important lever, though, is not your audience targeting at all - it's your creative. You want ads that really appeal to your target audience of people looking for plastic surgery, and really *don't* appeal to your *not* target audience of people who are not interested in plastic surgery.

Creative-led targeting and Non linear targeting pair perfectly together, especially when you have audience targeting restrictions in place.

B2B Targeting

The challenge that a lot of B2B advertisers face is how to ensure you're only reaching people who are part of a qualified business audience. For example, if you help large enterprises launch ecommerce stores, you probably wouldn't want to just advertise to anyone searching for "launch ecommerce store" because the vast majority of them will be looking for a B2C solution like Shopify, not a 6-figure solution like yours.

The first thing to keep in mind before jumping into any kind of B2B targeting strategy is that businesses are made up of *people*. Although you're trying to reach a certain kind of person who works in a certain kind of role at a certain kind of business, at the end of the day, you're advertising to a *person*.

When trying to target B2B, start by thinking through a day in the life of your target customer. I don't mean, "My customer persona is Decision Maker Dave who has 2.5 kids..." - no. Pick a real person who you would think of as being your ideal customer, and try to imagine what a typical work day is like for them. Or, perhaps you can ask them directly.

Let's say I'm trying to reach someone who owns a small- to medium-sized digital marketing agency, where they offer SEO and website development services, but don't have in-house Google Ads expertise.

This is a real customer persona for my Inside Google Ads course and Google Ads Coaching, and I have a particular coaching client in mind right now that I'll use for this exercise.

Okay, what does a typical day look like for this client? He lives in Australia, he runs the agency with his partner. From what I can gather, they specialize in serving home services businesses, and they seem skilled and competent in SEO and website development. New customer acquisition is pretty straightforward for them with local businesses, and they have good systems in place to execute an SEO strategy. They've been relying on white label freelancers for Google Ads, and that's why they came to me: the freelancers aren't cutting it, so they want to learn Google Ads and bring PPC management in-house for their clients.

What do I think this business owner does when he first wakes up in the morning? I know that he keeps odd hours, so I'd imagine that he's the kind of person who picks up his phone and checks his email before he even gets out of bed in the morning (for what it's worth, I'm one of those people, too). I'm going to keep that in mind for my strategy.

I know he watches Google Ads content on YouTube, since that's how he heard about me. I think he probably consumes a lot of digital marketing news and education sources: newsletters, podcasts, videos. I can see him checking that stuff throughout his day, and I'm going to keep that in mind for my targeting strategy, too.

He works from home, as many agency owners do these days, so there's no commute. There's probably not a lot of work/life separation, since his partner also works in the business. That means there are likely bursts or micro-moments throughout the day where he has specific problems that need solving, and I would expect Google Search and YouTube Search to play a big role there. Add that as an interesting point for my strategy.

I know that he's embraced ChatGPT in his agency, using it for ideation and draft copywriting. That tells me he's someone who embraces change, embraces new technology, and that he prioritizes efficiency. That will help me with my targeting strategy as well.

I could keep going, but you get the idea. By analyzing one specific person, one customer you know, you can glean so much more insight, and more *accurate* insight, than making up some avatar persona that doesn't really exist.

What have we learned that we can use to inform our B2B targeting strategy, from approximately 3 minutes of effort?
- Audience targeting clues: Small business owner, interested in digital marketing news and education, forward-thinking technologist, expert in SEO and website development
- Content targeting clues: Topics, Placements and Keywords related to digital marketing industry news, Google

Ads feature announcements, Google Ads tutorials and troubleshooting, SEO news
- Ad format clues: Gmail, Google Search, YouTube, Display

Imagine what you could learn with 30 minutes of effort.

The golden rule for business-to-business targeting is to remember that *businesses* don't buy products and services. *People* buy products and services.

Also remember that the person who *buys* your product or service may not be the same as the person who *uses* your product or service. For example, you may sell a SaaS product that automates a specific task for PPC managers. The person who will use your product is a PPC manager at an agency or in-house at a company, so you'll want to advertise to them and show them how your product will make their life better. But in order to buy your product, they'll probably need to pitch and get approval from the head of the agency, or the head of their procurement department. It may make sense (or may not make sense) to have a separate targeting strategy in place for those "purse string holders."

Your targeting strategy template

Your offer	Your target audiences
Targeting ideas: 1. How can I sell [offer] with Google Ads? 2. How can I reach [people] with Google Ads?	
Targeting restrictions?	
Audience targeting	**Content targeting**
Your data segments Google's data Custom segments • Searches • Websites • Apps Combined segments Automated targeting solutions	Search keywords Display/video keywords Topics Placements
Creative ideas: Why should [people] buy [offer]?	

Privacy, cookies & industry changes

I DIDN'T WANT to write this chapter. In fact, I still don't. This is one of the absolute last things I'm writing before sending this off to my interior layout designer.

Not because it's not an important topic - it is, and that's why I'm powering through for you! - but because Google Ads has always been simple, and this privacy stuff is not

That may seem like an odd and perhaps even incorrect thing to say, especially at this point in this book. Google Ads = simple?

To my brain, the way Google works has always been reliably, beautifully simple. Keywords. Bids. Audience layers. Formats. Give the machine what it wants, it spits back what you need. Our challenge as Google Ads practitioners is figuring out the best way to give the machine what it wants, so that we can get back what we need.

In contrast, privacy and cookies and pixels are all so messy and in flux. You will find plenty of well-written articles about the "Cookieless future" or "Beyond audience targeting" but the truth is, even Google doesn't know where this is all headed. Heck, Google told us for years that third-party cookies in Chrome were going away, only to reverse course in 2024 to say "Actually, we're keeping third-party cookies for now... but we're still trying to figure out how to *not* rely on them anymore."

The purpose of this chapter is not to predict the future, but to prepare you for it. I'm not here to make you an expert in how marketing technology works, just to give you what you need to know to keep managing your ads effectively.

Before diving into what's changing in our industry, let's ensure we understand the basics of how the digital advertising industry has been working so effectively for decades.

Because if you think about it, digital advertising wasn't just the first medium that allowed us to target audiences. It was the first medium that allowed us to precisely measure the ROI of our marketing dollars. There's an often-repeated quote from a retail magnate in the 1800s, "Half the money I spend on advertising is wasted; the trouble is I don't know which half."

No retailer would share this sentiment today. We may not be able to account for every single dollar (and we may have to start getting used to accounting for fewer of those dollars), but we can now pretty accurately measure the "last click" return on investment of most of the ad dollars we spend in digital.

The reason we can measure where our ad dollars are going and how they convert is cookies and pixels.

Cookies & Pixels 101

A cookie is a small file on your device that contains encrypted information about you. It is placed on your device by a website you've visited. When you visit certain websites online, they may "drop" a cookie on your computer so that the next time you visit, they'll recognize you.

For example, when you go to a website and you're still logged in from your last visit, that's thanks to cookies. When you visit an ecommerce website and they have the items in your cart from when you visited a week ago, that's thanks to cookies.

A pixel is a small piece of code on a website that tracks your behaviour. When you visit certain websites and take certain actions, the pixel on that site will send information about the cookie(s) on your device back to its mothership, a server.

For example, when you go to a website and add something to your cart, the pixel will look at your browser, say "Hey, I know that cookie! I left it here last week!"

Then, it will relay that information back to the server. I imagine it would say something like, "Earth to Server, Cookie ABCD123 has now added shoes to their cart. I repeat, Cookie ABCD123 has added shoes to their cart!"

Now, this website can hold those items in your cart, show ads to you tomorrow to remind you that those shoes are in your cart, etc.

If the pixel doesn't find any of its cookies on your computer, it will say something like, "Ooooh, we got a new one! Hey there Cookie XYZ456, go forth and hang out with the other cookies on this browser. Remember those shoes. Hopefully, I'll be back for you soon!"

This all sounds like a streamlined system, right? Well, cookies aren't as delicious as they sound, which is why they're going away.

☑ **Remember this: Cookie vs. Pixel**
A **cookie** is placed on your computer by a website, so that it can identify you in the future.

A **pixel** is installed on a website by the website owner, and drops cookies to keep track of users. It sends this information back to a server.

The problem with cookies

While cookies have been a boon to the advertising industry, they've got a lot of problems, too.

Cookies are device specific, so they can't account for cross-device behaviour. For example, researching something on your phone and then completing the purchase on your computer; that would involve two separate cookies on two separate browsers, so the business wouldn't know that these visits came from the same person.

Cookies are also not the most privacy-safe feature. It's very easy to hijack your cookies, or for any website to view and read your cookies and learn a ton of stuff about you.

Some web browsers have already banned third-party cookies, and Google kept saying that Chrome would do so, too, but that has yet to happen.

This is why you'll hear industry folks talking about a "Cookieless future," which was supposed to be here by now. But alas, it turns out it's pretty complicated to find a suitable cookie replacement.

Google is actively testing a variety of methods across web and Android to meet these conflicting goals: keep user data safe while enabling advertisers to drive business results, therefore keeping content free. It's called The Privacy Sandbox.

It's both a noble and self-serving goal, and it's not going well. For now, we've still got cookies. You can read more about it, if you're so inclined, at privacysandbox.com

How to win with Google Ads today

While the future of third-party cookies is hazy, the future of first-party data is not. The PII that *you* have about *your* customers is one of your greatest competitive advantages, your great edge in the ads auction, your holy grail of marketing nirvana.

Hyperbole? Yes. But only slightly.

In a world where every advertiser has access to the same bidding algorithms, and every advertiser has access to the same automated targeting algorithms, there are really only 3 things left that you can use to outperform your competitors.

Helpfully, they all start with the letter C:

1. Creative
2. Conversion tracking
3. Customer list

When you put compelling, unique creative into your campaigns, you get a higher click-through rate than your competitors, higher Quality Score, lower ad costs, and more robust data to feed your targeting algorithm.

When you're uploading your offline conversion data into Google Ads, your bidding and targeting algorithms get smarter about who to target next, and how much to bid for them.

When you upload your customer list into Google Ads, the same thing happens once again: your bidding and targeting algorithms get smarter about who to target next, and how much to bid for them.

We covered the full range of Customer Match benefits earlier in this book. As we wrap up our exploration of audience targeting in Google Ads, I cannot underscore enough how integral your customer data is to achieving outstanding Google Ads results today and in the future.

And you don't need to take my word for it. We know that Google focuses its ads product and engineering resources where they will have the most impact. Recent launches driven by first-party data innovation include conversion-based customer lists (using your PII), Google Engaged audiences (using Google's PII) and Confidential matching, a new feature that lets you use Customer Match through an encrypted, super-secure, privacy-safe process called confidential computing.

The features and functionalities of Google Ads will continue to change, but the foundation remains remarkably unchanged. Work with automation, not against it, so that you can turn the power of Google into the wind beneath your wings. If I could sum up what you need to do to win with Google Ads, in just one sentence, it would be this:

Feed the Google Ads machine what it needs (creative, conversion tracking, customer data) so it can give you what you need (customers).

☑ Remember this! 3 durable ways to outsmart your competitors in Google Ads

1. **Creative:** Craft headlines, descriptions, imagery and videos that appeal to and engage your target audience (and don't appeal to your *not*-target audience)
2. **Conversion tracking:** Implement full-funnel conversion tracking so Google Ads can optimize for your business' goals
3. **Customer data:** Leverage Customer Match to inform your targeting and bidding algorithms, so you can attract the most profitable users for your business

PRIVACY, COOKIES & INDUSTRY CHANGES

That's all, folks.

Inside Google Ads AI policy

IN TODAY'S EVER-EVOLVING digital landscape...

I'm kidding. I hope you can tell by now that this book was written 100% by me and 0% by AI. I thought very carefully about if and how to use AI in my book writing process, and wanted to share that thought process with you here. We're all getting used to these new tools, and as a Google Ads user, I'm sure this is on your mind as well.

I did not use AI to research, write or edit any portion of this book.

I also do not use AI to research, write, record or edit my Inside Google Ads podcast or Inside Google Ads course.

For book ideas and structure, I relied on my decade of experience with Google Ads, including 6 years at Google and 4+ years as a Google Ads Coach, Teacher and Content Creator. I have seen thousands of Google Ads accounts, advised thousands of marketers and business owners, and spent countless hours reviewing Google Ads documentation (both internal and external) about how this stuff works. That's how I knew there was a book's worth of information, insight and analysis about audience targeting.

To fact check, I consulted the Google Ads Help Center, my personal Google Ads account, my clients' Google Ads accounts, and trusted industry colleagues. My source for specific facts, like "the Display network has 3 million websites and apps," is always Google's public-facing Help Center, unless otherwise noted. If I'm unsure or unable to corroborate something that I believe to be true, I've made it known to you. Where none of these sources had a definitive answer, I went straight to the source and asked Ginny Marvin, Ads Liaison at Google. Thank you Ginny!

For editing, I relied on the generosity of my great friend Amalia Fowler, and my experience as a Copy Editor for the school newspaper at Tufts University. I only joined the copy editing team because I had a crush on the guy who ran it, and although that crush turned out to be unrequited, the skills I gained there have been immensely useful throughout my career, and especially in writing and editing this book. Thanks, dude!

For design, I hired an experienced cover designer and interior designer. He has not used AI in any parts of his process, either.

When it comes time to promote this book, I may use AI tools to create marketing materials like blurbs, descriptions, blog posts, etc. just as I use these tools to help *promote* my podcast and my course.

But everything you've read between the front and back cover was written by a human: me.

Acknowledgements

THANK YOU TO my parents for raising me to know that I am smart and special and capable of achieving anything. I'm so lucky to have you as my mom and dad.

Thank you to my children for your laughter and love. I love you both so so so much. Only one of you is old enough to read this sentence right now, so Nora - I see you! Great job on your reading.

Thank you to my husband for being my partner and supporting my ambitions.

Thank you to my brothers for making me tough.

Thank you to my colleagues at Google for challenging me and guiding me and teaching me the foundations of Google Ads. I never planned for this career, but I'm so grateful for it. Thank you especially to Eric for seeing potential in me and challenging me to get off my ass and do better; to Kirsten for being the best work partner I've ever had; to Giulia for being the first one to make me actually open up AdWords (as it was called then); and to Alanna for being there through the best days of my life, the worst days of my life, and everything in between.

Thank you to the #PPCChat community for friendship, knowledge and camaraderie. I wish I had found y'all sooner.

Thank you to the PPC Baddies group chat for keeping me sane, providing great advice and support and helping me know I'm never alone.

Thank you to Amalia Fowler for becoming the best friend I didn't know was missing in my life. Your time, expertise and care in providing me with feedback on early drafts were invaluable and encouraging. My life has been richer since you became part of it.

Thank you to Navah Hopkins for your unwavering friendship, support and mentorship. You have opened so many doors for me, I am eternally grateful - and the best door was the one that moved us from social media acquaintances to true friends.

Thank you to Tod Maffin and Darian Kovacs for supporting me from the beginning of my entrepreneurial journey.

Thank you to Raush Salhi for being my right-hand woman and keeping the business (and this book project) moving forward. I would be lost without you.

Thank you to Ginny Marvin for graciously answering my obscure questions, to ensure I published a thoroughly verified and fact-checked book.

And last but not least, thank you reader for trusting me with your time, your money and your Google Ads training. All three are privileges I take seriously and gratefully.

Thank you.

Made in the USA
Monee, IL
13 June 2025